Archaeology Data Service

GW01048807

CAD: *A Guide to Good P.*

Archaeology Data Service

CAD:
A Guide to Good Practice

Harrison Eiteljorg II, Kate Fernie,
Jeremy Huggett and Damian Robinson

with an additional contribution by
Bernard Thomason

Oxbow Books 2003

Published by Oxbow Books for the Arts and Humanities Data Service

ISBN 1 900188 72 4
ISSN 1463 - 5194

A CIP record of this book is available from the British Library

Cover illustration © Jeremy Huggett.
A computer reconstruction of the medieval timber and earthwork castle
at Symon's Castle, Powys

This book is available direct from

Oxbow Books, Park End Place, Oxford OX1 1HN
(Phone: 01865-241249; Fax: 01865-794449)

and

The David Brown Book Company
PO Box 511, Oakville, CT 06779, USA
(Phone: 860-945-9329; Fax: 860-945-9468)

or from the website
www.oxbowbooks.com

Printed in Great Britain by
Information Press, Eynsham, Oxford

Contents

Acknowledgements

The *Arts and Humanities Data Service* would like to offer sincere thanks to Autodesk and to the Royal Commission on the Historical Monuments of England (now English Heritage) for the financial contribution that they made in bringing this Guide to publication. Sincere thanks are also offered to those who have contributed to it by reviewing and commenting on draft versions. These people include:

- Richard Beacham, University of Warwick
- Adrian Brown, English Heritage
- Steve Dobson, University of York
- Rachel Edwards, Worcestershire Archaeological Service
- Jim Everett, University of Glasgow
- Mike Evans, English Heritage
- Nigel Fradgley, English Heritage
- William Kilbride, Archaeology Data Service
- Gordon Malcolm, Museum of London Archaeology Service
- Paul Miller, UKOLN
- James Purcell, Autodesk
- Julian Richards, Archaeology Data Service
- Hinda Sklar, Architects' Association
- Laura Templeton, Worcestershire Archaeology Service
- Keith Westcott, Archaeology Data Service
- Alicia Wise, JISC

Thanks are due to Worcestershire Archaeological Service for permission to reproduce the figures in Section 2.4.1.

The authors and editors of this Guide would also like to extend their thanks to all those who have worked so hard to bring it to publication. These people include:

- Tony Austin, Archaeology Data Service
- Jo Clarke, Archaeology Data Service
- Catherine Hardman, Archaeology Data Service
- Val Kinsler, 100% Proof
- Maureen Poulton, Archaeology Data Service

Section 1: Introduction

1.1 AIMS AND OBJECTIVES

This *Guide to Good Practice* is designed specifically to provide guidance for individuals and organisations involved in the creation, maintenance, use, and long-term preservation of CAD-based digital resources in the humanities.

The results from *Strategies for Digital Data*, a recent survey by the Archaeology Data Service of digital data in archaeology (Condron *et al.* 1999, 29–32), show that a wide variety of organisations are both creating and holding digital project archives. Increasingly CAD files and three-dimensional CAD models comprise a unique component of these archives and one which it may not be possible to reproduce on paper. Much of the functionality of the dataset relies on it being available digitally. For this reason the *Guide to Good Practice* is aimed at:

- **Creators of CAD files**, including contracting and consultancy units, university-based research projects and national and local societies
- **Agencies and bodies commissioning CAD work**, including national heritage agencies and local authorities
- **Curators who will receive digital project archives**, including museums, National Monuments Records and county or regional Sites and Monuments Records.

This guide is intended to provide:
- a basic description of computer-aided drafting or computer-aided design (CAD) software
- discussions on the use of CAD in a variety of situations
- descriptions of data acquisition and capture methods used
- good practices in the use of the software, and information about archival practices with CAD files.

In addition, there is a glossary of terms used in this Guide and in CAD generally.

As well as providing a source of useful generic information, the guide emphasises the processes of long-term preservation, archiving, and effective data re-use. As a result, the importance of adhering to recognised standards and the documentation of essential pieces of information about a given resource are dominant recurring themes.

In outlining the aims of the document, it is important to state what the current guide does not cover. It does not aim to be an exhaustive introduction to the underlying origin, theory and technical implementation of CAD. Nor is it in any way a definitive and prescriptive manual on how 'best' to do CAD. The aim of the guide is to introduce practitioners to areas and issues for which applicable standards and frameworks already exist and to identify the relevant sources of information that may be consulted. The guide does not rigidly advocate any single standard or narrow set of options, nor does it recommend any particular software product. Instead, it adopts a generic approach, with the aim of encouraging and developing the routine use of standards and data frameworks as a whole. In this sense it is important to realise that the present document constitutes a *guide* as opposed to a *manual*.

1.2 OTHER GUIDES IN THE SERIES

This *Guide to Good Practice* is one of a series published by the Arts and Humanities Data Service. The *CAD Guide to Good Practice* is one of a family of theme-specific guides, commissioned by the Archaeology Data Service. Taken together, these guides comprise a comprehensive, authoritative and highly complementary set of practical guidelines:

- Archiving Aerial Photography and Remote Sensing Data
- Digital Archives from Excavation and Fieldwork: a Guide to Good Practice. First Edition
- Digital Archives from Excavation and Fieldwork: a Guide to Good Practice. Second Edition
- Geophysical Data in Archaeology: a Guide to Good Practice
- GIS: Guide to Good Practice

The Arts and Humanities Data Service caters for digital archiving needs across the humanities disciplines of archaeology, history, literary studies, performing arts, and visual arts. Other AHDS service providers also commission *Guides to Good Practice* in this series and collaborate in their production. The Archaeology Data Service and the Visual Arts Data Service have jointly commissioned:

- Creating and Using Virtual Reality: a Guide to Good Practice (forthcoming)

Other Guides in the series:

Title	Subject area
Creating and documenting electronic texts	
Developing linguistic corpora	Textual Studies
Finding and using electronic texts	
Digitising history: a guide to creating digital resources from historical documents	History
Mapping History: A Basic Guide to GIS for Historians	
Creating digital performance resources	
Creating digitised audio materials for use in research and teaching	Performing Arts
Digital Collections in the Performing Arts: Metadata, Management and Minefields	
Creating Digital Resources for the Visual Arts: Standards and Good Practice	
Using Digital Information in Teaching and Learning in the Visual Arts	Visual Arts
Investing in the Digitisation of Visual Arts Material	

Table 1: Other Guides to Good Practice *from the Arts and Humanities Data Service*

The most up-to-date information on the other Guides in the AHDS series is available online (http://ahds.ac.uk/guides.htm).

1.3 HOW TO USE THIS GUIDE

Ideally any individual or institution involved with, or planning, a CAD-based exercise with the long-term aim of depositing the resultant data with a digital archive should read the guide in its entirety. In many cases, practitioners will only be dealing with one particular aspect of the overall potential of CAD, and to reflect this the guide has been structured into clear thematic sections. Individuals are advised to read the sections relevant to the task at hand carefully.

Throughout the sections, information is listed which it is critical to record if a well-documented CAD data file is to be produced, and to ensure that the resources produced can be effectively archived and re-used via the ADS or another digital archive. For clarity, this information is presented as a number of bulleted lists within the main body of the sections, but it is important to realise that all stages in the process should be documented – from project planning, survey and digitisation to modelling and publication.

1.3.1 Pathways through this guide

The following sub-section contains some suggested documentation pathways. These relate to tasks undertaken by different individuals or organisations involved either in planning or creating CAD survey drawings. In each case, a practitioner is identified and the relevant sections of the Guide are highlighted. The pathways presented are not intended to be exhaustive nor to be viewed as a prescriptive list. Tasks frequently overlap and it is often the case that individuals involved in undertaking the field-work are also intimately involved in project planning and archiving.

Practitioners are encouraged to use the pathways presented here as templates to develop their own 'good practice' check-lists.

Specifying a brief
- Sources of CAD data (Section 3.1)
- Choosing CAD layering scheme (Section 4.3)
- Acceptable data formats (Section 4.5)
- Specifying a digital archive (Section 7.1)

Planning a project
- Planning for the creation of digital data (Section 6.3)
- Choosing CAD software and hardware (Sections 4.1 and 4.2).
- Choosing a CAD layering scheme (Section 4.3)
- Contacting a digital archive (Section 7.2)
- Managing digital data (Section 6.4)
- Survey, data density and CAD (Section 3.3)
- Digitising techniques (sub-section 3.6.2)

Capturing data
- CAD data formats (Section 4.5)

- Choosing CAD software (Section 4.1)
- Precision and accuracy (Section 3.2)
- Storing digital data (Section 6.4)
- Documentation (Sections 5.3, 5.4 and 5.5)

Preparing to deposit an archive
- Contacting a digital archive (Section 7.2)
- Determining the metadata required (Section 6.6)
- Describing the archive (Section 5)
- Acceptable deposit formats (Section 7.4)

1.3.2 The thematic sections

To enable practitioners to target the individual sections most relevant to the particular task at hand, the aims of each section are summarised here:
- Section 2 provides a brief introduction to CAD, including how CAD programs have developed, important features of the ways that CAD can be used and its relationship to drawing programs, virtual reality and GIS. The aim of this section is to provide a contextual background to CAD in archaeology and architectural recording.
- Section 3 looks at common sources of data for CAD models, including field survey and data capture from maps, plans and photographs, and looks at the twin issues of precision and accuracy.
- Section 4 describes methods and techniques used in preparing CAD models including transferring survey data, creating CAD layers and naming conventions, choosing CAD hardware and software and CAD data formats.
- Section 5 looks at the procedures and considerations involved in planning and documenting CAD projects. This covers project design, specification, methodologies, preparing to model, segmenting the model into layers and the documentation required at each stage.
- Section 6 describes the need for good working practices in managing CAD (and other digital data) both during the working life of a project and in archiving the data. The concept of using metadata for resource discovery to safeguard CAD products for future re-use is introduced.
- Section 7 contains practical descriptions of how to go about depositing CAD models with a digital archive.

This Guide also includes a carefully selected set of bibliographic references and a glossary of terms.

Section 2: A brief introduction to CAD for the Humanities

2.1 AN INTRODUCTION TO CAD

Computer-Aided Design (CAD) software is used worldwide by designers, architects, surveyors and others. It is used in a wide range of applications, from producing designs for roads, office buildings and industrial prototypes to producing special effects for films and plans for electrical supplies and other utilities. It is now widely used throughout the arts and humanities, for example in building and site recording; archaeological survey; interpretative modelling, visualisation and reconstructions.

There are several important reasons to consider using CAD:

- The use of layers in a CAD model makes it possible to record complex material in a way that enables analysis and gives the flexibility to produce a number of views of the model showing different aspects of the material
- CAD models can be rotated to view a structure from different aspects
- Dimensions of data points can be retrieved from a CAD model at any time with the same precision used to take the original measurement, whereas in a scaled drawing the original measurements have to be re-calculated
- Data may be attached to items in CAD models, making the combination of CAD model and textual data more powerful than either alone
- CAD files may be used by many other program types, such as GIS and virtual reality programs, to provide the base data for other applications.

CAD can be used to create simple, two-dimensional drawings or to handle more complicated three-dimensional objects. This section will look at:

- How CAD has developed
- Important CAD features, layers, wire-frame, surface and solid models
- Rendering surfaces
- Multiple CAD files and connected data tables
- Differences between CAD, drawing programs and virtual reality
- Relationships between CAD and GIS
- Examples of how CAD has been used at the Acropolis in Athens, Deansway in Worcester and Symon's Castle in Powys.

2.2 HOW CAD DEVELOPED

CAD programs initially mimicked the world of two-dimensional paper drawings, but with the advances in both computer hardware and software, designing in three dimensions has became more and more widespread. CAD programs have an interesting parentage that helps to explain why they work as they do and which has bequeathed specific qualities to contemporary users.

2.2.1 Paper drawing conventions

Paper drawings of objects are two-dimensional representations of the real world and such technical drawings use a series of conventions. For example, engineering drawings generally show the front, right side, and top of an object (see Figure 1). Broken lines are used to indicate lines that are hidden in the particular view, another line type is used to indicate the centre of a circle, another for the longitudinal axis of a cylinder and so on.

Figure 1: Two-dimensional engineering-style drawing of child's block with inset letters on six faces

Archaeologists and architectural historians also developed a series of drawing conventions to indicate meaning when recording real world objects. For example, hachured lines are used to indicate the steepness of a slope on a plan, specific line types are used to indicate wear marks on drawings, etc.

2.2.2 Pin-bar drafting

A process known as *pin-bar drafting* was developed by architects to permit convenient draughting of multi-storied or very complex buildings. Multi-storied buildings have identical exteriors for many floors but might have different interiors. Similarly, complex buildings, whether multi-storied or not, required separate electrical plans, plumbing plans, plans for heating and air-conditioning ducts, and so on. To eliminate duplication of effort, architects could draw the structural outline of the building (and common features like elevator shafts) on one sheet of paper, position a transparent sheet over the base sheet (on registration pins, hence the term), and then draw the interior of a specific storey on a transparent overlay. In the same fashion, electrical diagrams, plumbing diagrams, and so on could each be put on a transparent sheet, and a large number of such individual overlays could be put together on the registration pins so that many drawings could be viewed at once – making all features or only a few visible at one moment, as required.

2.2.3 Computer-assisted drafting and Computer-aided design

Computer-assisted drafting (CADD) programs were developed for architectural use and given capabilities such as layering (see sub-section 2.3.1), mimicking the transparent overlays used in pin-bar drafting so that traditional architectural practices could continue.

Computer-aided design (CAD) programs were developed for engineering, to make it possible to move directly from product design specifications to manufacturing and to permit the visualisation of products in advance of production.

2.3 CAD PROGRAMS AND IMPORTANT CAD FEATURES

CAD programs are used to create a model of the real world. The term **model** is used in this guide to refer to the product of a CAD project, that is a computer file which can be re-used to create many individual drawings. The term **draw** will be avoided in this Guide because it implies the process of making a single drawing rather than the more flexible and complex digital product of a CAD project.

CAD software is widely used for two-dimensional drafting but most CAD software is now capable of creating three-dimensional models, complete with all the complexity of the real world. Whether a model is two-dimensional or three-dimensional it will be a complex layered version of the object under study.

2.3.1 Layering

CAD programs enable the parts of a drawing to be held in **layers** which can be displayed or suppressed on demand. The separate drawing layers created by CAD practitioners can be spatially, temporally or conceptually distinct from one another. For example, in Figure 2 different CAD layers have been used to hold different materials.

Using layers to build up a model is a crucial part of the successful application of CAD to problems in the humanities. Layers can be used in a variety of ways, for example:

- In archaeology different layers might hold materials from different phases or time periods
- In historic building survey, the masonry of a wall may be shown on one layer, the windows on another, doors on another, and roofing on yet another. Different layers can be

used for original parts versus additions, and any missing pieces might be reconstructed on yet another layer
- In theatre design, the different parts of the set may be shown on different layers – for example the stage, the flats, the designs for the scenes painted on the flats, the props and so on.

A thoughtful design of the layering system is one of the most important parts of creating a good CAD model (see Section 4.3, Appendix 2 and Appendix 3). This segmentation into layers makes real analytical use of the model possible and the way that the model is constructed has an enormous impact on the kind of analysis that can be done. Of course, the analysis of CAD layers differs from the types of analysis that can be done with GIS layers (see Section 2.9).

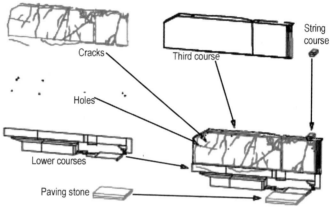

Figure 2: The use of CAD layers for different materials

2.3.2 Full dimensional precision

Early design systems developed for engineering needed to hold precise dimensions, which were passed to machine tools and used to cut parts. The locations of all points had to be maintained in the computer file as real-world coordinates so that the tool could determine exactly where to cut a part. The computer display was scaled so the user could see the drawing, but underlying the display remained real-world numbers.

CAD programs developed for engineers separated the display of drawings from the underlying numeric data. Modern CAD programs also hold the coordinates and measurements for the data-points used to create models in separate data tables. CAD models at different scales may be created from the data-points without the precision of the original data being affected.

2.4 TWO-DIMENSIONAL MODELS

The difference between two-dimensional drawings and two-dimensional CAD models is that a drawing offers a single representation of the world while a model may be structured into layers that can be viewed together or separately. In addition a model can be produced on paper at virtually any scale. A two-dimensional CAD model (such as Figure 4) may look similar to a two-dimensional drawing of the same plan but in fact the model offers much more flexibility. A series of different views can be produced from the model highlighting different layers. With thoughtful structuring of the CAD layers it is possible to use the model for analysis. For example, the locations of features with given characteristics (e.g. period, phase, material) can be compared, as is illustrated in the Deansway case study below.

2.4.1 Case study: Deansway by Jeremy Huggett

Major excavations on four sites in the centre of the city of Worcester were undertaken between 1988–1990 and revealed an extensive series of deep, well-preserved archaeological deposits which included evidence of Roman industrial activity and burial, an early medieval 'dark earth' deposit, a complex of medieval and post-medieval rubbish and latrine pits associated with tenement buildings fronting the main road, and the remains of a 15th century bronze foundry with bell pit. From the beginning, the importance of an efficient and flexible computer system was recognised. Particular emphasis was placed on the post-excavation process, although it rapidly became apparent that the computers had a much wider impact in terms of general illustration, display and education work, finds processing, site planning, staff development and public relations (Huggett 1989; Templeton 1990).

As is common practice in the UK, a single context planning system was used on site. Each context, representing any single event or action, was given a unique identifying number and individually planned, photographed, excavated and recorded. At Deansway each individual context plan was digitised into its own drawing file which was given the context number as its file name.

Planning conventions were used to ensure all context plans were drawn in a similar way. A series of line conventions were used to signify top and bottom edges of features, cut edges, temporary edges, and indefinite edges, for example. Similarly, standard formats for the inclusion of context numbers, level points and grid points were used.

A small number of basic layers were used to structure each drawing:

- 'Levels' used for level point symbols and associated values
- 'Contexts' used for context symbols and associated numbers
- 'Notes' used to annotate plans
- '0' default AutoCAD base layer, onto which all other drawn elements were placed.

These layers separated drawn elements from annotations and other textual elements, allowing plans to be merged without major conflicts. The use of layer 0 for drawn elements might cause problems because it is the default layer and it is easy to add to or edit this layer inadvertently. For this reason it might have been better if the drawn elements had been placed in a named layer in the Deansway model. Some additional layers would also have been useful so that top and bottom edges of cuts, for example, could have been differentiated.

Given the thousands of context drawings involved, it was vital to ensure that a completely consistent approach to digitising was adopted. A base prototype drawing was set up which acted as a template for creating context plans. This contained the necessary layers and line types, and also referenced a set of program functions and modified menus which were created with the aim of simplifying the creation of a digitised context drawing. Aids were developed to make it easy for draughtspeople to make the drawings and to maintain consistent styles. For example, menu options allowed the easy conversion of digitised lines to the type and colour prescribed in the convention and facilitated the insertion of pre-defined drawing elements, such as North arrows and formatted drawing title, scale, and location information. Other options, called small AutoLISP programs, were used to automate more complex functions – for instance generating level points with their values and placing grid point symbols with coordinate values (Huggett 1990).

This configurability was one of the reasons AutoCAD was used in the first place, and the value of this decision is shown in the way that today, over ten years after the system was first implemented, the same menus and functions have been migrated through several versions of AutoCAD without modification. The customised interface and associated functions also greatly simplified the training of new users, and enabled consistency of plans not only within a single site but amongst several sites.

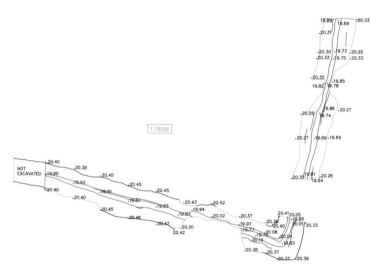

Figure 3: Plan of a ditch context at Deansway. (© Worcestershire Archaeological Service)

Once the digitisation of a context was completed, a function was provided to ensure each plan was saved in the same state. A record was automatically written to a data file which included the context number and coordinates relating to the extents of the context.

Since the internal coordinates of AutoCAD were mapped onto the Deansway site grid, different contexts can be brought together with ease and automatically positioned correctly both relative to the grid and each other, either as blocks (copies of contexts) inserted into an overall plan, or as cross reference files, i.e. links to the original file enabling changes to individual context plans to be reflected in the area plans (see Section 2.6 below). A number of tools were created to simplify this process; for example one AutoLISP routine took lists of contexts from Microsoft Excel and allowed them to be plotted automatically.

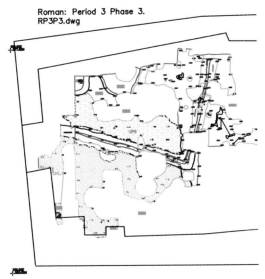

Roman: Period 3 Phase 3.
RP3P3.dwg

Figure 4: Part of a period/phase plan from Deansway, incorporating the context in Figure 3 inserted as one of a number of context blocks. (© Worcestershire Archaeological Service)

The primary emphasis at Deansway was the investigative value of this process. Context plans were combined to create Context Groups, Context Groups could be combined to create Activity Units and Activity Units combined to create Phases, all based on the same context-level drawing files. The composite structure and phase plans generated were used as draft plans which were originally inked by hand for publication, though improvements in technology make this unnecessary today. The overall methodology established by the Deansway Project has proved extremely robust over the years and remains in use. Modifications to the original methodology for subsequent projects include the definition of additional drawing layers in order to structure plans in a more flexible manner, and a greater emphasis on the use of polylines rather than freehand sketched lines. This simplifies subsequent modification within AutoCAD and also aids re-use in external packages such as GIS.

2.5 THREE-DIMENSIONAL DRAWINGS AND MODELS

The difference between a two-dimensional drawing and three-dimensional drawings or three-dimensional models is enormous. Figure 1 shows a two-dimensional engineering drawing of a child's wooden block with inset letters on each face. An isometric drawing of the same block (i.e. a drawing showing its three-dimensional nature without foreshortening the sides of the block as they recede) is shown in Figure 5. Most people would find the isometric drawings easier to understand than the engineering drawing.

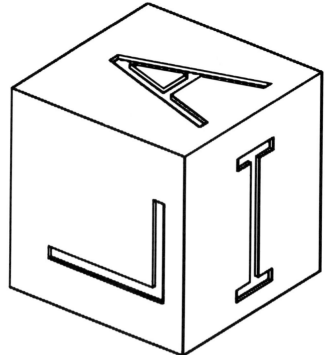

Figure 5: Three-dimensional isometric drawing of child's block

There are essentially three ways of constructing three-dimensional models in CAD:
- Wire-frame modelling
- Surface modelling
- Solid modelling.

Different CAD packages implement these to varying degrees.

2.5.1 Wire-frame models

A wire-frame model consists simply of points and lines drawn in three-dimensional space. These define the edges of objects, but there are no defined faces or surfaces. Figure 6 illustrates that these models can be very difficult to use. For example, it can be difficult to tell which lines in a wire-frame model are at the front and which are at the back from a particular viewpoint (the Necker cube effect). A wire-frame model of the older propylon on the Athenian Acropolis would be even more difficult to understand.

Wire-frame models should not be confused with the wire-frame representation of three-dimensional models which have defined surfaces. Surface and solid models may be viewed in CAD software as wire-frames for speed of viewing and manipulation.

Wire-frame models can provide the basis for other kinds of models. For example, the edges of complex objects can be precisely digitised as a collection of wire-frames and subsequently have surfaces applied to them or be converted into solid objects. For example, Figure 7 is a

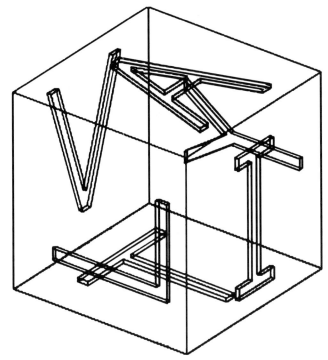

Figure 6: Wire-frame version of child's block

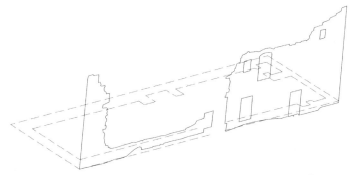

Figure 7: Wire-frame version of castle wall

wire-frame model of part of a castle, derived from an elevation drawing and placed on the floor plan. There is no solidity to the model, it exists only in outline as a series of interconnected three-dimensional points.

2.5.2 Surface models
Surface models are more complex than wire-frame models – as well as defining the edges of

Figure 8: Small surfaces used together to make a single, larger surface

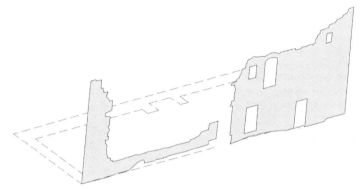

Figure 9: Surface model of the castle wall, derived from Figure 7

objects, the surfaces of the objects are also defined. Hence Figure 5 is a drawing based on explicitly defined surfaces to give the appearance of their real-world shape. These surfaces are opaque so that the lines and faces that would not show in a real-world view are suppressed (a hidden line drawing) – compare Figure 5 and Figure 6. An important CAD feature is that when asked to produce a drawing from a specific vantage point, the program can calculate which lines and surfaces should not appear in the drawing because they would be hidden by intervening surfaces.

There are many ways of creating surfaces, though in most cases these involve combining small surfaces to create larger, more complex objects. One method involves the construction of small, discrete surfaces that are then combined to make more complex objects (see Figure 8). These may be constructed as wire-frames and surfaces fitted between the edges. For example, Figure 9 shows the same model of a castle wall, but this time the edges have had a (greatly simplified!) surface fitted between them. As a result, when hidden line is applied, the wall now looks more solid.

A combination of these approaches is to create templates for surfaces, which can then be swept along pathways to create more complex shapes. For instance, a wire-frame cross-section of a pot could be swept through 360 degrees to create the inner and outer surfaces of the complete vessel. Similarly, Figure 21 (a Digital Terrain Model of Hambledon Hill) is an example of a surface constructed by linking together an array of three-dimensional points to form a mesh (see Section 3.4.6).

An alternative method is to use the CAD program's ability to construct standard geometric solids (boxes, cones, spheres, etc.) automatically, which provides the components that make up the overall shape. Virtually any regular geometric solid can be constructed by most CAD programs and assembled (by Boolean operations of addition, subtraction, etc.) to create more complex solids, a facility that is widely used in design. However, the real world is not made up of regular geometric shapes and recording real-world objects usually requires the construction of large, complex surfaces from small, simple ones. These small surfaces must lie in a single plane; therefore the simplest surfaces are triangular as three points may always be placed in a single plane. Even if a CAD program permits construction of more complex irregular surfaces without using individual planar facets, small surfaces are crucial when modelling very complex geometry.

2.5.3 Solid models

Surface models are constructed from the faces of an object leaving the interior of the object undefined or hollow. In a solid model the composition of the interior is defined – hence it is solid. Although in most views a solid model seems identical to a surface model, a CAD program can produce a cross-section through it. Solid models are created using boolean geometry – adding, subtracting, and 'differencing' simple shapes to create more complex ones. In general, solid models are easier to work with than surface models. For example, it is topologically difficult to cut a hole in a surface mesh, but it is easy to 'carve' features out of a solid model by subtracting elements from each other. Furthermore, materials can be assigned to solid models and their properties analysed – for example, the mass and centre of gravity of an object can be calculated or its load-bearing capacity determined.

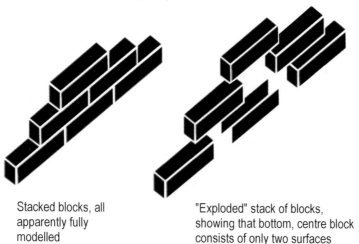

Stacked blocks, all apparently fully modelled

"Exploded" stack of blocks, showing that bottom, centre block consists of only two surfaces

Figure 10: An apparently solid model of a wall

The central block in the middle of the wall depicted in Figure 10 consists of only two visible surfaces. However, all six sides of that stone would need to be surveyed for a solid model to be created. In Figure 11, the original surface model of the wall has been extruded to create a

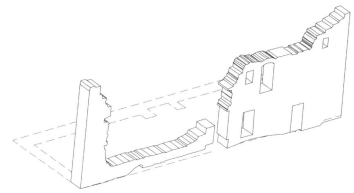

Figure 11: Solid model of the castle wall, derived from Figure 9

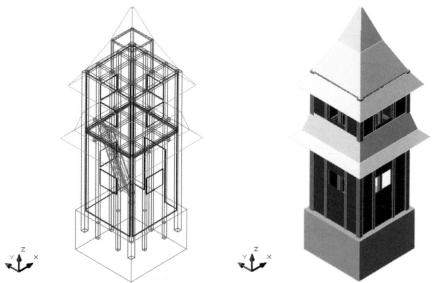

Figure 12: Solid model of a timber tower (wire-frame and shaded representations) (Huggett and Chen 2000)

solid wall, and the windows have been created by subtracting them from the wall. The same effect would have been very complex to achieve using a surface model.

Solid models are also commonly created using a standard 'toolkit' of geometric shapes – boxes, wedges, cones, spheres, etc. – which are again combined using boolean algebra to form more complex shapes. For example, Figure 12 is a solid model of a timber tower, which, apart from the roof, is created entirely from boxes using boolean addition and subtraction.

The value of visualisation in public presentations is being increasingly recognised in the humanities, especially in archaeology and architectural history. At the same time, three-dimensional modelling tools are increasingly found in even relatively basic CAD packages. However, it is important to be clear about the purpose of such models. For example, the wall in Figure 11 is a greatly simplified representation of the real world, and while it may provide an adequate visualisation it is far from accurate. It is, however, simple to construct, manipulate, and, with the addition of appropriate surface textures, can provide an effective small-scale model. On the other hand, a fully detailed solid model can rarely be made without dismantling standing structures and the gain from creating such a highly detailed model is often minimal. Such models are complex to make and demanding of computer hardware and are generally only used to address specific structural questions. For example, they might be used in reconstructions of missing structural elements of an historic building, such as in the reconstruction model of the Roman baths in Bath, where the heights and cross-section of the masonry vault were remodelled as a result of the application of physical principles to the solid model (Lavender *et al.* 1990).

Programs may permit some cross-over between techniques, and users should be familiar with the processes before beginning to build an important model. Learning the intricacies of CAD modelling is best done with one's own objects and survey data than through any tutorial or sample process. Trying to match real geometry requires the user to understand it at the outset and have a sense of what a good finished model should look like. Although regular solids (boxes, cones, spheres, cylinders, etc.) can often be created with a CAD program, easy-to-use creation tools are rarely useful for modelling real-world objects.

Figure 13: Model of the older propylon which has been rendered with complex textures and shadows to create a reastic impression of stone walls, steps and of the floor.

2.5.4 Rendering

Technically, rendering refers to the process whereby a model is displayed on screen from the associated data files. However, the term has come to be used specifically to refer to the process of applying colour, texture and so on to the surface of CAD models. A series of sophisticated processes has been developed for CAD software to illustrate the appearance of objects. These are used to study the results of design choices that affect appearance, e.g. colour, texture, and subtle changes in shape. These programs are particularly important for designing consumer products and in reconstructions, as they enable models to be given a real-world appearance. For example:

- Lighting can be adjusted to see objects under different conditions
- Surface treatments can be applied, e.g. the child's block could be treated to appear if it were made from wood with white paint to highlight the letters
- Surface textures can be applied, e.g. a photograph can be used to create a bitmap which is applied to the model giving a real-world appearance.

The use of CAD software to render a model allows more 'realistic' reconstructions of archaeological monuments. For example, the tower in Figure 12 has been rendered using basic colours and shading, while in Figure 13 more complex textures have been applied. The realistic appearance of such images, however, can be deceptive if read uncritically (Eiteljorg 2000).

2.6 MULTIPLE CAD FILES

With large projects, such as an archaeological site or building complex, a single CAD file may become cumbersome and difficult to manage. The issue is the size of the file as the bigger it is the slower computer operations become. It may be better to create separate CAD files for the individual elements that make up a large project. Links can then be established to cross-reference the files (often called cross-references or xref files) to one another creating a composite model. Any number of CAD files linked in this way can be displayed together as if they are part of a single model. Although only one CAD file can be edited at any one time, any changes will be reflected in the composite model.

An advantage of using cross-referenced files lies in the ability of the CAD practitioners to work on small files as they create the elements that make up a large model. Different people may work on different parts of the model at the same time. There are also disadvantages, as editing common aspects of a group of files is more time-consuming than making the same edits in a large file. It is also important to make sure that the layer-naming convention is consistently applied across all of the linked files.

It can also be advantageous to use cross-referenced files for elements whose copyright owner is different from that of the rest of the model, for example where a map is used to provide a background to a plan in a two-dimensional model. The model may be viewed with the element where copyright permission has been granted, e.g. in a publication. The copyright restricted element may be removed prior to distribution, e.g. when the model is deposited in an archive.

The most significant problem with using multiple CAD files is maintaining the links when files are transferred to a different computer or to a digital archive. If links are established by explicit directory pathways that are specific to the host computer (e.g. c:\projects\pompeii\ 2000\p211.dxf), when the files are moved to a new computer the links no longer point to the files. Secondary users must re-establish the links between the files by specifying the correct directory pathway. An alternative method is to specify relative directory pathways (e.g. ..\..\p211.dxf), which may ease the problem of moving linked files to a new computer; however, files must be copied in their directories with all relevant sub-directories to maintain the relationship. In addition, some CAD packages enable collections of drawings to be gathered together into projects. Changing the project's search path can also facilitate the exchange of drawings between users, or deal with different drive mappings to a server location. It is important to document the relationships between cross-referenced files, particularly when depositing a CAD project in a digital archive (see Section 5.6).

The key issues in considering the use of cross-referenced files is the size of the files and how the elements of the model will be produced. There is no rule of thumb; CAD practitioners will need to experiment with their models to see if they have become too large for current equipment. If speed is not a problem, using cross-referenced files offers no benefit to the end user except where the files are being worked on individually. In that case, it may be desirable to model the individual elements and then to copy these into a single composite model for distribution to others.

2.7 CONNECTED DATA TABLES

Some CAD programs allow users to connect individual items within a model to additional information held in external data tables. Such information might include simple annotations or detailed information about items in the model. For example, the individual stones in a building might be connected to a data table that specifies material, date of construction, surface textures, tooling marks, and Munsel colour.

The data table may be linked directly to an element in the model or a layer may be created in the model containing icons. These icons can then be linked to an external file containing explanatory notes. For instance, notes about the prior use of a specific group of blocks, or the blocks used in a certain wall, could be attached to an icon – perhaps an arrow pointing to the blocks in question.

Connecting CAD models to external data tables gives an opportunity to expand on the information in the model or contained in the layer-naming system. Such links are two-way connections and they can add useful analytic capabilities. For example, starting with the database one might obtain the set of all the re-used blocks and then highlight those blocks in the model to display their distribution. Considerable use may be made of such capabilities in excavation recording and intra-site studies, for example by linking context and artefact files to site plans.

There is a significant problem with using data tables connected to CAD models. At present, the technology offered by CAD programs to connect data to CAD models is proprietary and has changed from one version to the next. As a result, the database connections made from CAD files are often broken when the file is migrated to more recent versions of the CAD program. The use of a non-proprietary format to create the connection should enable data to be moved from one digital file format to another without fear of data loss. One such non-proprietary system for connecting data tables to CAD files is described in Eiteljorg 2002a. As CAD technology develops, the severity of this problem may diminish but it is unlikely to disappear overnight.

2.8 CAD, VIRTUAL REALITY AND OTHER DRAWING PROGRAMS

CAD files may be passed to other kinds of programs to be used in different ways. Two of those program types, rendering software and virtual reality software, have the potential to transform the rather prosaic line art of a CAD model into startlingly lifelike images. CAD files may be passed to drawing programs to produce final publication standard illustrations with appropriate labels and graphics. It is important, however, that CAD should not be confused with virtual reality, or vector and raster drawing programs.

2.8.1 Rendering software

Rendering software provides tools to add surface materials, textures, and colours to CAD models. In addition, lighting – even the light of the sun in a particular place on the globe – can be simulated, complete with reflections, shadows, and more subtle effects of reflected light. The results can be realistic views of structures, images that make such structures come to life for the viewers. Rendering software has become so popular that CAD programs often include good rendering tools, but the best renderings are produced with specialised rendering programs.

2.8.2 Virtual reality

The other kind of program for producing more realistic views, virtual reality software, has received a great deal of attention in the archaeological community. It has the potential to take photorealism to another level, creating virtual worlds with all the effects of rendering programs plus the ability to mimic moving through or around the model, seeing it from any angle and watching things change as the viewpoints change. Stereo views are even possible. Although the promise of virtual reality software has been recognised for some time, the computer power needed to provide the best level of verisimilitude and the ability to move freely in three-dimensional space is not yet widely enough available to provide high quality results outside research laboratories.

   CAD models are often used as the basis for many virtual worlds. The virtual world used in a VRML model, for example, can be described as a series of coordinates in a text editor. Such a process, however, is difficult and time consuming and it is best to develop the world initially as a CAD model and then to convert the CAD model into VRML using a convertor. The CAD model should remain the core data source for archaeological materials. For more information about Virtual Reality, see the *Virtual Reality Guide to Good Practice* (forthcoming).

2.8.3 Painting and drawing programs

Drawing programs and paint programs are also sometimes confused with CAD. However, there are important differences which are most significant when comparing CAD and paint programs.

   CAD programs store lines, arcs and circles using mathematical formulae (vectors) so that they can be represented at any scale, on screen or on paper, at any time. While **Paint programs** permit users to draw lines, arcs, and circles, they store the results as individual dots (pixels or rasters). Once drawn the results are only isolated, independent dots that cannot be understood as composing larger entities. Enlarging or reducing such drawings often results in computer images with jagged lines in some places and blotchy, unclear shapes in others. Editing such drawings must be done one dot at a time. These programs are not designed for line art, nor are they able to deal with precise dimensions unrelated to the scale of the drawing.

Drawing programs are closer to CAD programs as they also use vectors to store drawings. However, unlike CAD data, the vectors are not tied to real-world numbers. Instead, they are related to the drawing page and are scaled implicitly. Furthermore, the three-dimensional features are very limited. These programs are capable of making excellent presentation drawings, using CAD output as the starting point, but they lack many of the precision and three-dimensional features of CAD programs.

Both paint and drawing programs lack some of the features that can make a CAD model so much more complex than a drawing or illustration – when CAD files are passed to any of these programs (rendering, virtual reality, paint or drawing) it is generally without the layers and attached data tables that give CAD models their flexibility.

2.9 CAD AND GIS

Geographic Information Systems (GIS) have some similarities with CAD programs in that they represent spatial objects that are linked to data held in tables. GIS software was developed for geographers, cartographers and others working with maps and, of course, maps have some similarities with architectural plans. While GIS can incorporate scanned paper maps or digitised vector maps, early versions in particular offered only limited drawing facilities. CAD programs are much more sophisticated in this respect and, as a result, they are often used to create maps that are imported into GIS. These factors have encouraged confusion about the differences between CAD and GIS programs. Despite that confusion, they are very different in terms of their aims, offer different features and have very different internal data structures.

CAD systems were developed for representing geometric objects. These objects can be described in more detail by tabular data that is attached to the CAD model. For example, it is now possible to attach an element in a CAD model to the data in an external data table (see Section 2.7). However, the aim is descriptive: the data simply augment the geometric representation of objects with additional information beyond that which is implied by its shape, position and layer designation in the model. For example, an artefact in an excavation may be shown in a CAD model and linked to additional data that describe its material, surface treatment and so on.

GIS can incorporate a series of different maps (vector and raster) linked to data and overlying one another in layers or coverages. GIS emphasises the link between a graphic object (a feature such as a point or defined area on a map) drawn on a layer or coverage and associated data. The graphic object and data can be taken together as parts of a set on which the GIS can perform mathematical and other functions. GIS offers considerable powers of analysis both within and between sets. For example, a GIS could find all settlement areas that were associated with a particular type of sherd. These results could then be compared to another set to find which of those settlements were located on a particular type of soil. In addition, GIS includes many features that allow interpretations of and calculations based on terrain, such as calculations of the steepness of a hill or of the areas that can be seen from a specific vantage point.

In short, the connection between spatial information and tabular data is more robust and more central to the functions of GIS than CAD; the resulting analytic possibilities are therefore much greater. However, GIS cannot be used to model complex three-dimensional objects adequately, such as buildings or excavation trenches. Although height data can be recorded in GIS, no point can have more than a single elevation and at best 2.5-D effects can be produced. For more information about GIS see the *GIS Guide to Good Practice* (http://ads.ahds.ac.uk/project/goodguides/gis/).

Many projects can benefit from the use of both CAD and GIS, although the distinction between the two can be expected to disappear as CAD features are increasingly added to GIS software and GIS features are added to CAD software, driven by commerical interests. In the meantime, the Symon's Castle case study (below) illustrates the use of both CAD and GIS, emphasising where GIS departs from CAD.

2.9.1 Case study: Symon's Castle by Jeremy Huggett

Symon's Castle is a 13th century motte and bailey castle on the Welsh borders. Over a ten year period (1985–1994) the total excavation of both the bailey area and the motte top was undertaken in a joint research project between the Archaeology Department at the University of Glasgow (J. Huggett) and the Continuing Education Department at the University College of Wales Aberystwyth (C. Arnold).

Computerisation was undertaken off-site out of season, and included the generation of topographic survey data, a context and artefacts database, and two-dimensional stone-plans and three-dimensional artefact plots created using AutoCAD. On-site equipment limitations meant that all coordinate data, whether for artefacts locations, topographic survey, or context recording, were recorded using basic level and tapes. Tests and estimates showed the resulting accuracy to be within ±100mm.

The nature of the site was such that individual contexts were rarely identifiable except in areas that had experienced severe burning – elsewhere, the shallow, leached soil meant that colour differentiation was absent. Major differentiation in stone was apparent, but otherwise structural evidence was extremely slight with few earth-fast timbers. The primary structural evidence consisted of artefacts – the motte-top excavation, consisting of a relatively small area of less than 22 metres by 27 metres, produced over 10,000 individually recorded artefacts, some 3,000 of which are fragments of burnt daub. Many of the burnt daub fragments bear the impressions of wood grain on their flat surfaces, and a number of fragments are characterised by several flat surfaces, either stepped or at right angles to each other. These are interpreted as being derived from horizontally planked timber-framed structures that were caulked on their inner faces with daub. In addition, nearly 700 nails, around 1,200 fragments of lead, and 500 pieces of medieval pottery were found, plus the usual smattering of less common items – some loose change, some buckles and some ironwork, including knife blades and arrowheads, for example.

During excavation it became quite clear that the two-dimensional location of artefacts was significant, but only in the sense that locations of types of material became predictable and the suspicion developed that this was related to the presence of otherwise invisible structures. AutoCAD was used initially to generate artefact plots related to stone plans (for example, Figure 14) and across the area of the motte as a whole (Figure 15), with different categories of artefact plotted on different layers and in different colours, enabling combinations of material to be viewed at will. However, this was not as useful a means of visualisation as had been

Figure 14: AutoCAD plot of the stone plan of the tower area of the motte, with lead distribution superimposed

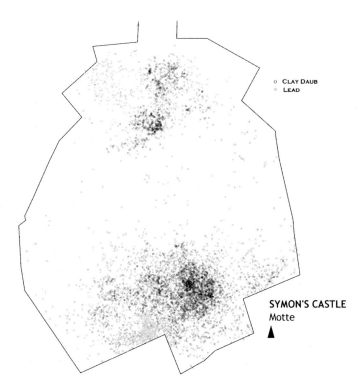

Figure 15: AutoCAD plot of the motte excavation with lead and clay daub distributions superimposed

expected since the density of artefacts overwhelmed the plots. There were simply too many items to make an ordinary distribution plot meaningful, beyond the observation of some extremely large concentrations. Yet this information was vital to the understanding of the layout, organisation and nature of use of the site, given the lack of structural evidence.

A more analytical means of handling the data was clearly required; specifically a means of calculating summary data according to different criteria and presenting the data in a more meaningful manner. This level of analytical requirement exceeded that available within a typical CAD system (although add-ins for some packages are available as extras), but is well within the capability of a Geographical Information System. In this case, the existing CAD data – plans and artefact distributions – were exported as DXF files for import and manipulation in the IDRISI GIS package.

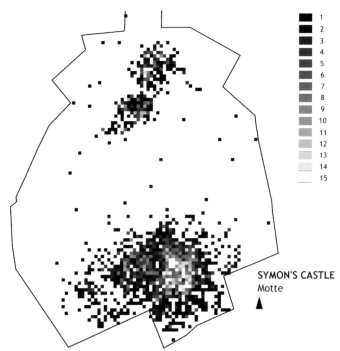

Figure 16: An IDRISI-derived incidence matrix based on counts of clay daub within a 0.25m grid across the motte

Given the need for resolution and interpretability, contouring was rejected as a technique, as, depending on the interval chosen, patterning was too diffuse or too inexact to be meaningful in terms of the identification of structures and activity areas. Instead the point data was rasterised within the GIS to form incidence matrices for artefact categories which enabled clearer patterns and distinctions to be identified by generating artefact counts within 1 metre, 0.5 metre, 0.25 metre or smaller grid squares (Figure 16). At a basic level, this provided a visualisation method at a range of resolutions which meant that the distributions were more amenable to examination and interpretation. The three-dimensional artefact data could also be used to construct cross-sections in the absence of identifiable context information, which could then be used to test theories about building location and destruction (Figure 17). The end result is the identification of the location of at least one building, and possibly a second, along with a probable cooking area, together with a greater understanding of the structural elements which did survive as identifiable contexts (Figure 18).

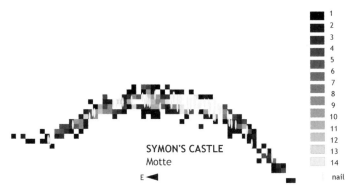

Figure 17: An IDRISI-derived incidence matrix based on counts of clay daub within a 0.25m grid constructed as a cross-section through a possible structure on the motte. A distribution of nails is plotted as an overlay

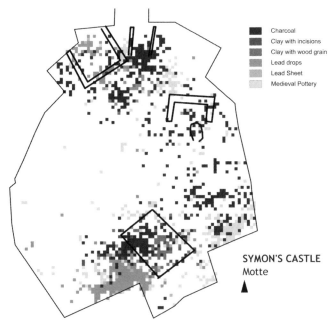

Figure 18: An interpretative plan showing the possible layout of buildings and associated structures combined with an incidence matrix of a range of artefact categories calculated on the basis of predominance within each 0.25m square

This example illustrates the potential interrelationship between CAD and GIS. The distinction between the two types of software is sometimes blurred by the incorporation of GIS or GIS-like add-ins to commercial CAD packages, but the basic differentiation between the kind of data handling and manipulation available within a typical CAD system and a GIS remains. In the CAD version, data were organised in layers which could be used to reveal or hide combinations of data as desired. However, a crucial element within the GIS was the ability to manipulate and combine layers mathematically, creating new categories of data for analytical purposes.

Section 3: Capturing Data for CAD Projects

One of the first decisions that must be made by the project director concerns the methods that will be used to capture data into the CAD model. This may involve a combination of field survey and digitisation or off-site data capture, yielding data with different levels of precision, and separate CAD layers or cross-referenced files may be created as the data are incorporated.

3.1 COMMON SOURCES OF CAD DATA

A range of different techniques are available to capture data for CAD projects. The most common sources of data for CAD models are:

- annotated lists of measurement points derived from traditional hand measurement survey techniques
- digital data logs derived from total station or GPS survey techniques
- digital data logs produced by direct object scanning
- digitisation of maps, plans and drawings
- digitisation of photographs, including rectification and photogrammetry
- existing CAD models.

The selection of an appropriate technique and methodology will depend on a number of factors. Project planning will involve careful consideration of both the object to be modelled and the type of CAD model to be produced and its uses. For example, a two-dimensional plan or elevation will require fewer data-points to be captured than a three-dimensional wire frame or surface model. A three-dimensional solid model will require even more data-points as both visible and invisible surfaces must be modelled.

Project directors must also consider the appropriate levels of precision and accuracy required for the project, the methods of survey to be used and the availability of maps, plans or photographs for digitisation. Before commencing data capture, project directors are recommended to select an appropriate CAD layer-naming convention (see Section 4.3).

3.2 PRECISION AND ACCURACY

In capturing spatial data into a CAD model it is important to consider at the outset the issues of precision and accuracy. These should be considered at the project design stage and the appropriate level of precision decided upon.

3.2.1 Precision

The **precision** of a measurement refers to how exactly that measurement was made and not the correctness of the measurement. For example, a measurement made to the nearest millimetre is more precise than a measurement made to the nearest centimetre.

The precision of a measurement is reflected in the number of significant (or meaningful) digits with which it is expressed. Thus, a measurement of a block of wood known to be 2.01034 metres long, expressed with two significant digits, is 2.0 metres. If the block was measured with a micrometer precise to a tenth of a millimetre we would show it as being 2.0103m long. If the same block was measured with a steel tape precise to the nearest millimetre the measurement would be 2.010m. The trailing 0 seems to offer no information, but in fact shows that the measurement is precise to the nearest millimetre. A measurement of 2.01m would be accurate to the nearest centimetre. For a detailed discussion about precision and the relationship to significant digits see Eiteljorg 2002b, chapter 2.1.

The high precision offered by modern instruments should be used, as a rule, since data can always be degraded but cannot subsequently be improved in precision. The precision of survey control points is of particular importance, as readings taken from a control point whose coordinates are given to two decimal places can only be given to the same level of precision.

3.2.2 Accuracy

The **accuracy** of a measurement refers to how correctly it was taken and not how precise that measurement is.

A measurement made at a low level of precision should be as accurate but not as precise as a measurement taken with a higher level of precision. Making certain that measurements are accurate should involve both calibration of equipment and repetition (see Appendix 1). Calibration tests the accuracy with which instruments measure while repeatability tests the efficiency of personnel and procedures and project directors should develop schedules for calibrating instruments, training and evaluating personnel and procedures.

To summarise, accuracy relates to the correctness of a result while precision essentially relates to the size of the smallest unit of measurement.

3.2.3 Appropriate levels of precision

Different levels of precision are appropriate for different projects, depending on the intended uses for the model produced. Modern survey methods make it easy to obtain very high levels of precision and there may be a temptation to seek the precision that is possible rather than that which is appropriate. For example, survey instruments like total stations automatically take measurements with high levels of precision. This can yield very misleading models; for example a rendered model illustrating a reconstruction of a building may imply that the original builders and craftsmen worked to very tight tolerances. The actual tolerances, however, are more likely to have been much looser.

For example, a project to record surviving concrete walls at Pompeii might decide that measurements should be taken to the nearest centimetre, but not to the nearest millimetre. In this case, higher levels of precision were not required, since the dimensions of the buildings measured to the finished surfaces do not survive. The concrete wall cores that do survive were not constructed to tight tolerances and measuring with great precision therefore provides no useful information.

Ancient cut-stone architecture that does not involve mortar, on the other hand, was constructed to very precise tolerances because of the absence of mortar and the unforgiving, inelastic nature of stone. The precision of measurement must be similarly high. In general the rule is that high levels of precision in construction and design need to be reflected in measuring the finished product. Lower levels of precision in construction, on the other hand, call for lower levels of measurement precision.

For paper drawings a more practical approach is matching appropriate precision to drawing scale so that the most precise measurements can be expressed in a drawing at the scale to be used (see also Section 4.4). Thus measurements are taken with the scale of the final drawings in mind, to the level of precision that would be useful in those drawings. Andrews *et al.* (English Heritage, undated) suggest that survey precision will be affected by the scale(s) at which surveyors expect drawings to be produced. This is certainly the case when surveyors are attuned to hand-drawing methods rather than CAD.

3.3 SURVEY, DATA DENSITY AND CAD

There are a number of factors which must be taken into account when planning a survey to capture data for a CAD model.

The first consideration is the object to be modelled and the end product that is required. An historic building, a barrow, an excavation plan, some theatre scenery flats and a garden plan each have their different aspects and might be modelled differently in CAD. However, the decision whether to undertake the work in two or three dimensions or to create a wire-frame, surface, or solid model is only partly based on the shape of the object itself. The product that is required also influences the decision. If plan views or elevations are required, then two-dimensional data may be gathered from the outset. An archaeological plan or plan of the standing remains of a building might be made with three-dimensional points but be treated as a plan only; a wire-frame model would be appropriate in such cases.

Similarly the number of data-points that are recorded will depend on the type of model that is being produced and the final product(s) that are envisaged, including any visualisation that is required. A three-dimensional model will have at least twice as many points as a plan (see Figure 19). For example, a wall must be surveyed as carefully where it meets the ceiling as where it meets the floor to produce a three-dimensional model, even if it appears to be vertical. An archaeological feature recorded in two-dimensional typically involves a quite dense collection of data points for the outline but relatively few points recording the depth or profile. Such a level of recording cannot subsequently be transformed into a reasonable representation of the original three-dimensional feature unless many more points are recorded in the first place.

Details within the structure being modelled also affect the density at which data are collected. For example, a wall made of cut marble blocks might require four points for each block while an irregularly surfaced mud brick wall might require a number of points along each edge as well as points spread throughout the surface.

The intended uses of the model should also be taken into consideration when planning the density of data collection. For example, a higher data density will be required if a three-

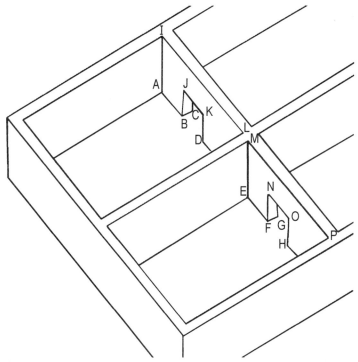

Figure 19: Survey points needed for two-dimensional and three-dimensional survey. Points A-H would be needed for a plan only, two-dimensional survey Points I-P would also be needed for a three-dimensional survey

dimensional model is to be used for renderings, virtual reality presentations or other presentations that aim to give a full sense of the object. The scale of the required output also influences the number of points being captured. For example, fewer points are required for a two-dimensional landscape output at 1:10000 than for a similar survey output at 1:1000.

Considerations of time and cost will also influence the type of model that is produced and the number of data points that are captured. When considering data density, practical choices must be made as every added data point complicates the model, the model making, and the end product. Every added point creates some additional costs. However, the value of the model may be compromised if insufficient points are taken because it may not be be possible to return to site at a later date. Even if it is possible to return to the site, capturing additional points at a later date represents a much greater cost than during the original survey.

3.3.1 Preliminary modelling

Preliminary modelling of portions of the object may be undertaken to test whether appropriate levels of precision are being achieved. Similar tests may also be undertaken to check whether data are being gathered at an appropriate density, e.g. checking the digital terrain model (DTM).

3.3.2 Case study: planning the survey for the Pompeii Forum Project by Nick Eiteljorg

The Pompeii Forum Project was planned with a CAD component from the beginning, as a major part of the work involved careful consideration of construction material, sequences, and processes. That being the case, and with the technology available when the project began in 1994, the plan included use of a total station and on-site CAD modelling.

The major focus is on the creation of a complete computer model for the east side of the Forum in Pompeii. (This work has required only one test excavation.) The model is intended as a major result in its own right and to illustrate many of the scholarly conclusions reached during the course of the project.

The 1994 season served mainly as a test for equipment and procedures to be used later. In 1995 new equipment was taken – a five-second total station (with five-mm EDM), two laptop computers with AutoCAD and data transfer software, and camera equipment for photogrammetry (non-metric 6 x 7cm camera and lenses). The work began in earnest that year.

There were some unusual requirements because of the nature of Pompeii:

- No stakes could be driven into the ground to provide datum points for surveying. One of the first jobs for each new area was establishing datum points on specific stones for future reference. For the 1996 season a special device was created to make it easier to establish datum points and to enable the survey crew to find those points again with certainty
- The volume of tourist traffic forced some compromises in terms of set-up positions and the length of working sessions
- The nature of the earth and the paving stones meant that set-up positions were often not stable. This frequently meant that the transit (level) could not be levelled and had to be moved
- The heat of the sun meant that the transit was rarely used for long periods at midday and the operator's hat was used regularly to shade it. Longer sessions would have required an umbrella for the total station.

Work began with a total station and prism on a pole, but holding the prism steady was more difficult than expected. When working with data points, the variation introduced was small enough to be ignored, but when setting up the datum points the problem was more significant. In the 1995 season a mini prism without a pole was used to achieve true stability. The close work that we were doing required care to make sure that the prism (mounted on a pivot) was pointing directly back at the instrument. Visual checks required hand and voice signals to communicate from the machine operator to the prism holder.

Plane transformations of photographs (or single-photo photogrammetry) were used for parts of the Sanctuary of the Genius of Augustus. Medium-format photographs were taken, including at least four markers that were positioned and surveyed in advance. The plane transformation process assumes a single flat surface. However, the surfaces were distorted and in some cases there were multiple planes at different distances from the camera, each having to be treated separately. The process was slow and difficult, particularly because data from the total station was combined with data from the photographs. A surface model was built with the total station data and it proved to be very difficult to add detail to that, since the data from the photographs assumed a single plane where no such single plane existed.

There were other areas where dimensions of details on walls were important for determining reconstructions. Standard tape measures were use to good effect there and also in areas that were inaccessible to the total station. It was necessary to do some triangulation, to survey elevations (of the floors and the wall tops) and both sides of door and window openings. Assumptions that surfaces are horizontal and/or vertical are rarely confirmed.

During the first two seasons survey work was done in the Forum during the day and modelling during the late afternoon and evening. Survey data came in too fast under that system, and the model lagged further and further behind, leaving survey data in the computer but unused until later. Once the project personnel had gone back to the real world, it was difficult to catch up. The schedule was changed for the third season; survey work stopped earlier in the day with more time devoted to building the model. It was then possible to keep building the model in tandem with the collection of data and while the sense of the place was still clear in the minds of the members of the working crew.

Layer naming has been a problem. It took some time to develop a system that was satisfactory, and several trials were rejected. Re-working the layer names after a good system was established tended to be put off. The system developed depended on room numbers established by the Project Director, John J. Dobbins, and another of the project members, Larry F. Ball, before work on the project had begun, with the CSA Layer-Naming Convention as the underlying scheme (see Appendix 2).

On more than one occasion the importance of good drawings of the survey work was brought home to the members of the crew. Generally speaking, the reminders were positive, but there were a few occasions when time was lost because of inadequate field notes or drawings. Modelling a structure with isolated data points is not as automatic as one might expect and the quality of the notes was crucial.

3.4 FIELD SURVEY FOR CAD MODELS

3.4.1 Hand-measurement surveys

Where moderate levels of precision are required, or on surveys of relatively small objects, traditional hand-measuring techniques may be appropriate. Steel tapes provide excellent precision and accuracy for short dimensions, longer dimensions inevitably introduce error from sagging tapes. Difficulties may also be experienced in measuring along oblique or curved surfaces, or along vertical lines, and so on. Determining longer dimensions by combining shorter ones creates different problems, since errors multiply.

All data-points in a three-dimensional model, of course, must have an elevation but triangulation becomes especially difficult when three-dimensional points are required. It is probably best to measure points in two steps, one to locate the position in plan view only, and another to determine elevation.

With hand-measuring processes, both note-taking to document the process and data gathering requires careful attention. If a three-dimensional model is to be produced more data points are required and these must be fully specified in all three coordinates. Line levels and plumb bobs will be needed to check the orientation on horizontal or vertical planes and, with inclined surfaces, measurements of the inclination are needed. Users should be certain that the geometry of the subject is fully specified; recording for three-dimensional modelling is much more demanding than recording for plans and elevations. It is easy to have a large number of data points with one or two crucial dimensions missing.

3.4.2 Total station surveys

A total station is an electronic theodolite with an electronic distance measuring device (EDM) and usually incorporates a data recorder or data logger. The advantage of these sophisticated surveying instruments lies in the precision that they produce for both long and short measurements. Other advantages of using a total station includes the speed of recording and digital data logging which combine to allow many more data points to be gathered at once in comparison with hand-measurement techniques.

The electronic theodolite displays swing angles (deviation from North) and the angle above or below the horizontal. The EDM sends an infrared beam to a reflector that must be positioned at the point to be surveyed and uses timing algorithms to determine the distance to the reflector. The data recorder records the position of the instrument, the swing angle, the elevation angle, and the distance to the target for each measurement. In addition, the data collector (and often the total station itself) can use simple trigonometric formulae to compute the position of a point surveyed from the known position of the total station and the horizontal and vertical angle and distance, generating a three-dimensional coordinate for the surveyed point.

Some total stations are now able to measure distance without a reflector, although they cannot necessarily make a reading from any surface (as the surface must reflect a significant portion of the light striking it). Therefore, even surveys using this sort of total station will occasionally need a reflector. Some problems are associated with using reflectors; for example, assistants are needed to hold the reflector and data points must be within reach (Eiteljorg 1994; 1995; 1996a; 1996b).

Total stations operate at various levels of precision. Some measure angles to the nearest five seconds, others to the nearest second. Some measure distances to the nearest 2 or 3 millimetres, others to the nearest millimetre with an additional potential error factor related to the size of the measurement. Selecting the correct machine is a matter of matching the expected working distance and conditions, the precision required, the machine capabilities, and price.

The potential error due to angular mis-measurement is very small when compared to the error that may occur in the distance measurement (see Appendix 1).

3.4.3 Transferring data collected from a total station to CAD

Data may be collected using a total station and transferred to CAD in two principal ways:

- **transferring data from the data logger incorporated into a total station into CAD software**. The points will be surveyed, and the coordinates transferred from the data logger to a computer and from there into a CAD model. The data consists simply of a group of numbered and annotated point coordinates and the operators connect the points to make a useful CAD model. Sketches are made on site just as they would be in a hand survey. Surveyed points must be noted so that the operators of the CAD system will know how to translate isolated data points into the surfaces, lines, arcs, and so on that are the CAD model

- **working with a total station connected directly to a computer rather than a data logger**. The computer may serve just as a data collector, in which case the system does not differ appreciably from a simple total system. However, the total station data may go directly into a CAD program in which case a CAD model can be generated interactively on screen during survey. With this type of system there is little requirement to make sketches on site during the survey.

When integrating data themes which are derived from survey data, the following should be recorded:

- The source (paper/digital map, GPS, data from mapping agency) and estimated error of survey base station coordinates
- Details of the survey, including date, time and purpose
- Details of the thematic organisation of the survey
- Make and model of instrument used
- Type of survey
- Estimated error terms for the coordinate pairs and (if appropriate) the z-coordinate
- Georeferencing information, overall accuracy of the survey data.

When transferring data from a total station or GPS the data points, two-dimensional drawing information and wire-frame lines will be brought into the CAD model. Building the model from the data points involves the following steps:

- The points are brought into the model, in their own layer(s), with numbers or other unique indentifiers
- The points are used to define points in model entities, lines, surfaces, etc.
- Both the original data points and model entities exist in the model
- The data points are no longer useful to the model and may be removed but should be archived for later re-use and accuracy checks. There are a number of options available:
  - The points can be kept in a frozen and hidden layer
  - The points can be brought into a parallel model, using the same grid system and explicitly related to the principal model, and kept there
  - The original transfer files created from the total station may be archived after discussion with an appropriate repository (see Section 7).

3.4.4 Case study: modelling the older propylon in Athens by Nick Eiteljorg

The survey of the older propylon to the Acropolis in Athens (the predecessor to the Propylaea, the classical building standing at the entrance today) began in 1975. CAD has been used on this project since 1986, with a number of different CAD techniques and programs being explored.

When survey work began in 1975 it was carried out with traditional measuring devices (levels, plumb bobs, tapes, carpenter's squares, etc.) and a series of elevations was taken with a transit (known as a level in the UK). It was clear from the outset that certain of the blocks were not vertical and, as a result, measurements of the inclinations of their surfaces were taken with a tape measure and plumb bob. Had those measurements not been taken, the construction of an accurate three-dimensional model would not have been possible.

Modelling work began in 1986 with a CAD program called CADDraft. A fully three-dimensional model was made with ARRIS, the first fully three-dimensional CAD program available for PCs, and it ran on Xenix, a Unix variant. The model was later re-created with AutoCAD, although many other programs were tried prior to this.

The survey data could not be entered as simple x-, y-, z-coordinates. Measurements were

Figure 20: The area of the older propylon on the Athenian Acropolis

always taken from some specified point or points in the structure to the one in question. As a result, new points always had to be defined in terms of other points in the model, not known locations in a Cartesian grid system; locating the points in the modelling process required relating a new point to one or more old ones. In some programs that was very easy but others proved more difficult to use either because they forced the use of the mouse or because only minimal tools were provided for specifying geometry from the keyboard.

When the model reached an advanced state, interpretation suggested that the rough fortification wall behind the propylon had been moved by tectonic forces and so the stones were surveyed. A desktop photogrammetry program called MR2 was used and this information made it possible to finish the model (Eiteljorg 1990).

When AutoCAD R12 was released connections between the model and a database became possible. This enables each *in situ* object to be linked to a table containing information about the material, date of erection and demolition, number of such blocks, etc. All objects were also linked to a table defining the layer names and their meaning, e.g. that a stone was *in situ* but in a secondary use setting.

Illustrations were prepared for publication (Eiteljorg 1993). These were made by exporting AutoCAD drawings to Adobe Illustrator where text and shading was added. The illustrations were then printed on film for direct inclusion in the printing plates. The CAD model has also been made available on-line by the Center for the Study of Architecture/Archaeological Data Archive (http://propylaea.org/).

3.4.5 Global Positioning System receivers

The Global Positioning System (GPS) is a worldwide navigation system based on the Navstar satellite constellation, which is designed and run by the US Dept of Defense. GPS is used for a wide range of applications including navigation, time coordination and surveying. A key concept in achieving accurate positions with GPS is that of differential positioning. If data collected at a fixed GPS receiver with a known position is used in conjunction with data collected simultaneously by a second, mobile, unit the accuracy of the positions recorded by the second unit can be considerably enhanced. This technique is applied over a range of equipment through the use of geostationary satellites, beacons, Ordnance Survey (OS) Active Stations or users' own base stations. Real-time GPS uses the constantly transmitted data to correct the position reported at the mobile receiver instantaneously, while post-processing systems collect data over a period of time from reference stations and moving units and then process it later.

GPS equipment falls into three broad bands:
- single units for navigation, without recourse to transmitted correction data, produce positions accurate to approximately ten metres
- code only units, usually characterised as GIS collection, or mapping grade, produce positions to better than one metre using broadcast beacon data
- surveying grade equipment uses a range of techniques to fix positions to within one centimetre and is used for large survey control schemes and geodetic measurement.

GPS derived positions are in latitude, longitude and height within the World Geodetic System (WGS84), or equivalent local geodetic systems such as the European Terrestrial Reference System 1989 (ETRS89). In order to use surveys on base mapping, the survey data must be transformed to the local mapping grid, in the UK the OS National Grid (OSGB36). Transformation to the National Grid can be done most accurately using the Precise National Transformation, which is accurate to 0.2m anywhere in the UK. This is available free on their website, or as a computer program and is incorporated in the latest versions of GPS survey resolution software.

Surveying using differential, dual frequency, real-time GPS equipment is typically carried out using a fixed base station composed of a GPS receiver with antenna and radio mounted on a tripod, or a vehicle such as a Land Rover and a rover unit carried by the surveyor in a back-pack or mounted on a pole. Available surveying techniques include the following:
- Surveying fixed points, high levels of accuracy (<5mm) can be obtained by larger occupation
- In kinematic mode the receiver can be set to fix points at a pre-set time or distance interval;
- Set in kinematic mode and either carried by the surveyor, or mounted on a moving vehicle, GPS equipment can be used to collect large numbers of three-dimensional points for landscape or terrain modelling. Such data can then be used for site interpretation or reconstruction, or for use in engineering design or for measuring erosion for conservation purposes
- Feature code libraries can be loaded into GPS data collectors, so that surveyed points can be tagged with appropriate codes. These codes can then be interpreted by survey resolution software and lines drawn between points on appropriate drawing layers and of predetermined colour and line-type.

The Ordnance Survey National GPS Network website at www.gps.gov.uk offers data from the Active Station network for post-processing with the surveyor's own dual-frequency GPS observations. This allows a surveyor with a single survey grade GPS receiver (base and rover) to determine GPS latitude and longitude at any point in Great Britain and replaces the need to visit at least three trig points to get a good transition from WGS84 to OSGB coordinates.

3.4.6 Case study: a GPS survey of Hambledon Hill by Bernard Thomason

Hambledon Hill, a major Neolithic and Iron Age settlement in Dorset, was surveyed at 1:1000 scale by the RCHME (Royal Commission on the Historical Monuments of England) in 1996. GPS surveying equipment was used on the site to survey the defences and to fix the position of the conventional graphical survey of the hillfort interior to the National Grid.

An advantage of using the GPS is that all the data collected have three-dimensional attributes, that is x, y and z coordinates. In addition to the detail points taken on the ramparts some 12,500 points were collected in a grid pattern within the hillfort and on the lower hillsides outside the defences. A Leica single-frequency roving unit was used to collect all the points while a similar receiver, acting as control or base station, occupied a nearby Ordnance Survey triangulation station. The roving unit was set to kinematic mode, that is it was set to record the three-dimensional position every five seconds as the surveyor walked backwards and forwards over the hill. Using GPS equipment meant that the relative accuracy of all the points collected was very high. The coordinate sets from the defences, the interior and the hillsides were then combined to create a computer-generated model that was in turn used to construct a contour plan and a digital terrain model (DTM) (Figure 21).

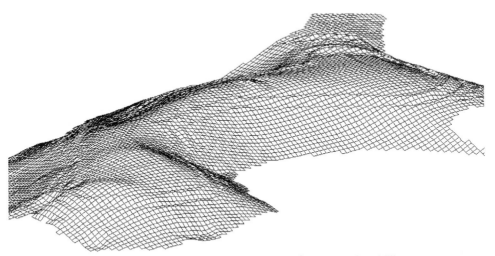

Figure 21: Digital Terrain Model of Hambledon Hill

The Digital Terrain Model (DTM) shown in Figure 21 is a surface model, i.e. it has no thickness and contains no volume. The DTM was created from a mesh calculated from the three-dimensional coordinate points. Survey data is typically visualised in this form.

3.5 DIRECT OBJECT SCANNING

It is technically possible to scan large objects and structures, just as it is possible to scan drawings (see Section 3.6). Many kinds of equipment, including mechanical, magnetic, and optical devices are available for this process but these tend to be expensive.

Devices that are suitable for scanning large objects are heavily automated and they often make the resulting models much more complex than necessary. This is because excess data points are collected, as the points surveyed depend upon a pre-defined grid rather than on logical choices of required points made by a surveyor. Software is used to reduce the number of data points by removing those that are not required – for example, points that are not at the edge of a large, flat surface. This process of 'decimation' (removing the excess points) is still improving (Eiteljorg 2002b).

It is very difficult to separate the data points collected by automated scanning processes into CAD layers. This is particularly true where large numbers of data points have been collected and they are not tied to specified points in the real world.

3.6 RETROSPECTIVE CONVERSION TO CAD FROM MAPS, PLANS AND DRAWINGS

Maps, plans and elevation drawings are the most widely available and commonly used sources which are retrospectively converted to CAD. There are four methods of entering data into a CAD system from these sources:

- measurement
- digitising
- 'heads-up' digitising
- semi-automatic tracing.

The process of importing information from maps, plans or drawings will have implications both for data precision and accuracy, and it is important to be aware of a number of issues. The first of these concerns the source material itself. While maps, plans and drawings that originate on special plastic films, such as mylar, are reasonably stable, paper can stretch and distort over time. In addition, where the item is a copy rather than an original a number of distortions may result from the copying process used. In general, the following information should always be recorded:

- Publisher and copyright owner, which will often (but not always) be the same. For Ordnance Survey mapping, the copyright holder is the Crown
- The medium
- Scale of the original source, given as a ratio, and the original scale (where the source map is an enlargement or generalisation from another source)
- Name of the original source, e.g. map and the map series (where appropriate)
- Claimed accuracy for any specific components: map makers will often provide an estimated precision for contour lines or other sub-components of a map
- All details of the map projection and coordinate system employed. This information is usually printed on the mapsheet or else should be sought from the map source.

Whichever technique is selected, it may be necessary to experiment with the original data sources to determine the levels of accuracy, precision and reliability that can be obtained by comparing dimensions on the original source with those in the CAD model (see Appendix 1).

3.6.1 Measurement

The information from the maps, plans or drawings can be used to provide the dimensions and locations of geometric shapes. Coordinate points are derived from the source and manually entered into the CAD package. The process is the same as making a model from a standard hand-measured survey. Assuming that all measurements are present, a full three-dimensional model can be created.

3.6.2 Digitising

Plans may be traced directly into a CAD package as vector data using a digitiser. A digitiser is an electronic drafting board that is used instead of a mouse to provide data input to a computer. Large digitisers are available so that even drawings of considerable size can be traced easily. Drawings of any size can be traced and properly orientated, working on a portion of the whole at a time, even on small digitising tablets. However, larger tablets save time when dealing with large drawings. Scale, position, and orientation are established before tracing, and the user has complete control over the tracing process.

Digitising tablets generally offer finite resolution in both x and y directions. This can be expressed as a quoted resolution, for example 0.02 inches or 0.001 inches, or as lines per inch (lpi), e.g. 200 lpi or 1000 lpi. This information can be found within the digitiser manual. Unlike the scanning process, where a scanned map generates a single raster image, digitising a single paper plan may form the basis of a large number of discrete, thematic vector data layers.

When digitising, the following additional information should be recorded. As with the scanning process this may involve careful checking of hardware and software documentation, for example to determine the resolution of the digitiser.

- Detail of the digitising device used, such as the make and model, software driver and version
- The precision, usually specified as a quoted resolution or as lpi
- Details of any automatic vector processing applied to the theme (such as snap-to-nearest-node)
- Details of control points used to manage conversion from digitiser to real-world planar coordinate systems
- Errors incurred in the above transformation process (e.g. quoted RMS).

It is possible to use plans and elevations together to create three-dimensional effects and, with some patience, three-dimensional models. If a plan view is traced, for instance, the elevation can also be traced, starting on the proper points on the plan but placed on a vertical plane. Of course, adjustments will be necessary to accommodate the deviations from simple, planar drawings, but such adjustments are possible in some, if not all, cases.

3.6.3 Heads-up digitising: a scanning-digitising hybrid

Another option is to create a scanned image of the source document and import it into CAD software. The CAD software used for this purpose must be capable of both importing and manipulating a scanned raster image.

Scanning

Maps, plans and drawings can be scanned, with a flatbed or drum scanner, to generate two-dimensional raster images. Scanning devices vary considerably in accuracy and resolution, with flatbed and drum scanners normally providing a resolution between 100 and 1200 dots per inch (dpi). The more expensive drum scanners claim resolutions of between 3–5000 dpi. In all cases care should be taken to distinguish between the true optical resolution of a given scanner and that obtained through interpolation procedures. If scanned, then there is likely to be a single raster file data product.

There is a very wide variety of image formats for holding raster data (e.g. TIFF, GIF, JPEG), the majority of which are designed for photographic images and not spatially referenced data. It should be noted that the scanning process can result in some very large raster images.

For products that have been generated by scanning paper originals, the following additional information to the core mapsheet data should be recorded for each raster file generated. It should be noted that to retrieve some of this information will involve careful checking of the respective hardware and software documentation:

- Details of the scanning device used, such as the make and model, software driver and version
- Parameters chosen in the scanning process, such as the resolution setting of the device, the number of bits per pixel used
- Details of any pre-processing undertaken on the source mapsheet. This may include a range of options provided by the specific scanning software used
- Details of any post-processing undertaken on the data, such as noise reduction or sharpening with convolution filters, histogram equalisation, contrast adjustment.

Heads-up digitising

Once the image has been imported in to the CAD software it is scaled to the correct dimensions and moved to the correct orientation and effectively it is registered in space. The image can then be used as the basis for 'heads-up' or 'on screen digitising'. This involves using the mouse pointer to trace around the elements of the image that are to be digitised. Coordinates are recorded as the mouse moves in much the same way as when moving the puck on a digitising table or tablet. A vector data layer is created and, once this is complete, the raster original is generally deleted from the CAD model.

The advantages of heads-up digitising include:

- The technique can be used when no digitising tablet is available
- Once the raster image has been orientated correctly in CAD it can be digitised in several sessions without the need for re-registration or checking the calibration of a digitising tablet. The ability to work in shorter sessions minimises errors that may result from fatigue, etc.
- As the image is displayed on the computer screen it is easy to zoom in to clarify complex

areas. The limit to which an image can be enlarged is the point at which the lines in the image become jagged because the individual pixels have become visible as squares or rectangles.

A typical desktop scanner scans at 300 pixels per inch and at this resolution each pixel represents approximately a 0.085mm square of the original image. Scanning at higher resolutions retains more detail in the image. It can be useful to scan at a slightly higher resolution than you intend to digitise because the image remains clear when you zoom into complex areas. However, as a general rule, images should be digitised at approximately the scale at which the vector data will be used. This is because although the vector data can be rendered at different scales, a fixed number of data points exist and if the scale is increased too far lines may become jagged. If the data are used at a much reduced scale, an unnecessary number of data points will have been recorded resulting in a large file size.

The disadvantages of heads-up digitising include:

- Large format scanners are needed to scan large originals and these may be difficult to obtain
- CAD software may not be able to correct all of the distortions in the original source material unless this is a two-dimensional drawing with all dimensions in the same horizontal or vertical plane.

3.6.4 Semi-automatic tracing

Raster images can also be made into vector data by using one of a number of software products. These include very sophisticated, semi-automatic, tracing tools which can vectorise 70–80% of the data for an ideal image without intervention. Such tools request intervention by a user when a problem, such as crossed lines, cannot be resolved automatically. They can manipulate the output from high (over 3000 pixels per inch) resolution drum scanners, as well as from desktop flatbed scanners. These programs are expensive, although they are sometimes available at discounted rates to non-profit research or educational institutions. Although there are also a number of cheap/shareware tools available for use on a PC, these have limitations in terms of the maximum scan resolution they can handle, or the size or complexity of the image.

Semi-automatic tracing programs create very large files owing to the number of separate line segments that are created. None of these programs can convert 100% of a scanned map or plan into vector data without human intervention. The amount of intervention that is required depends on the sophistication of the program, the quality of the scan and the complexity of the image. Without human intervention automatic tracing programs have limited usefulness as they become confused, e.g. by lines that cross one another. Nevertheless, cleaning and correcting an auto-trace may represent a considerable time saving over digitising a map or plan from scratch.

3.7 PHOTOGRAPHS

3.7.1 Digitising

The easiest data to obtain from photographs are details from flat surfaces, e.g., the pattern of a mosaic floor or the cracks on a wall. A single photograph can be placed on a digitiser and traced, just as if it were a drawing (see sub-section 3.6.2).

Unlike GIS software, CAD software does not include tools to rectify and georeference the raster images produced if the photographs themselves are scanned. For a detailed bibliography and for a full discussion of the issues and techniques involved, including scanning and rectifying aerial photographs, please refer to the GIS *Guide to Good Practice*.

3.7.2 Photo rectification

If photographs are taken at an oblique angle to the surface then photo-rectification software can be used to perform a mathematical process called a plane transformation.

Although CAD software cannot be used to rectify a scanned photograph, some CAD packages in combination with a digitising tablet can be used to trace and rectify details from a photograph in one step. However, the resulting trace will be a two-dimensional plan and assumes that the underlying surface represented in the photograph is flat, an assumption that may not be appropriate or reasonable in all circumstances. For example, an aerial photograph or elevation photograph may be placed on the digitising tablet, which is calibrated using at least six or more well-separated known two-dimensional coordinate points. As details are then traced from the photograph, they are automatically transformed into the underlying coordinate system. This provides a limited degree of 'rubber-sheeting' for oblique photographs. A series of statistics indicating the amount and location of error will typically be provided by the software and should be recorded as an indicator of the overall accuracy of the rectification.

3.7.3 Photogrammetry

Photogrammetry is a technique for producing scaled drawings or models from photographs. It requires photographs in pairs with a known distance between the two camera positions and very sophisticated equipment. Newer methods, often called close-range photogrammetry or desktop photogrammetry, use three or more photographs and various computer algorithms to locate positions of common points, i.e. points that can be identified in multiple photographs.

3.7.4 Incorporating photographs into CAD models

When incorporating photographs into CAD models the following information should be recorded:

- full photographic details
- details of the rectification method(s) used
- the software employed including, where possible, specific parameters chosen
- details regarding control points used in georeferencing.

3.8 CONCLUSIONS

Producing a CAD model will generally involve more than one method of data gathering. For example, total stations do not work well at very close range and they are cumbersome to use for small details. GPS is excellent for landscape survey but works less well for the details of standing architecture. Photogrammetry is difficult and expensive but excellent for details seen well in photographs. Tapes and traditional hand-measuring systems are slow but useful in areas that are inaccessible to total stations. Digitising existing plans, drawings or photographs allow existing data to be utilised. Each system has its drawbacks and each has its strengths.

When planning a data-gathering exercise a number of issues should be taken into account:

- Equipment, procedures and personnel should be kept under review to monitor the levels of precision and accuracy that are being achieved
- Where possible, modelling should proceed in tandem with survey work to ensure that data are being collected at the appropriate precision and density for the task
- An appropriate CAD layer-naming convention should be selected and followed (see Section 4.3)
- All factors affecting the collection of data should be fully and accurately documented (see Section 5). Potential users must be able to examine such documentation if they are to understand the quality of the data.

Section 4: CAD systems

This section looks at some of the differences between CAD packages and emphasises the importance of choosing a system that is suitable for the proposed task. Computer hardware and software are both developing and specifications change rapidly. When establishing a CAD system it is important to check that the components are compatible, including those elements that allow models to be viewed on other platforms such as the file format and layer-naming conventions used.

4.1 CHOOSING CAD SOFTWARE

The most obvious consideration when choosing CAD software is whether it will do everything that you need it to. Different packages have different capabilities and it is not always obvious whether a specific program will meet all the requirements for a given job or how easy it is to use for your purposes. For example:

Will the software accept data input from keyboard, mouse and digitiser?

- Users intending to use CAD for design should look for programs that ease data input using the mouse and the graphical user interface
- CAD users intending to input data points using the keyboard should experiment with programs to make sure that it is easy to enter absolute data points or define points in relation to others
- CAD users intending to enter data using a digitiser require an interface system that accepts input from the digitiser in place of a mouse and permits scanned drawings to be scaled, related and traced. Not all CAD software allows this, especially cheaper packages.

Some CAD packages automate the creation of regular shapes; irregular shapes create more problems. Different CAD software has differing capabilities for two-dimensional, three-dimensional wire-frame, surface and solid modelling. Not all CAD software can be connected to external data tables and this capability is an important consideration if it is intended to link site plans or models to materials, context or artefact data. Users should experiment with inputting typical data to be sure that the proposed system meets their needs and may wish to take advice from a colleague who is familiar with the program and the intended work.

Less popular CAD software may not support the full array of peripheral equipment and users may be restricted to specific graphics cards, plotters, or input devices which in turn may have limited availability or be expensive. With Windows and Macintosh systems, connections to peripheral devices do not normally depend on the CAD program; however, it is important to be certain that proper use is made of data from peripheral devices.

CAD software uses proprietary file formats and these do not necessarily transfer successfully between different programs (see Section 4.5). Users are recommended to check that the available file formats are appropriate for their needs. For example, drawings from a CAD model are often exported to illustration programs like Illustrator, Freehand, or CorelDraw where text and other features are added for publication. CAD users should check that the proposed program will be able to export files in appropriate formats and that an appropriate format for deposit with a data archive can be produced.

Those who are planning to use a total station for survey work should check the availability of a program to accept data from a total station and format it appropriately for the proposed CAD system. Data are often collected from a total station and converted to DXF files which may not transfer successfully into all CAD software.

CAD users should consider the medium- to long-term stability of the manufacturing company and arrangements for support, including the availability of training and instruction manuals for users. Commercial training in CAD can be very expensive and users may wish to consider the availability of alternative options.

Finally, more expensive CAD packages generally offer more facilities than cheaper packages, but these may not be necessary for the intended purpose. Users should check the facilities included against their requirements.

4.2 CHOOSING CAD HARDWARE

As computer hardware is developing rapidly and costs are going down, when choosing hardware it is important to check the minimum specification required to run a particular CAD program but then to check whether a higher specification machine is available. Software requirements will generally direct CAD users to IBM-compatible PCs rather than Macintosh computers or workstations using Unix, Linux or other operating systems. Factors which should be taken into consideration are processing power, RAM and the size of the hard drive. Working with large models (changing points of view, making hidden line drawings, rendering the model, etc.) requires a fast computer although the hardware requirements will be reduced if the model is solely in two dimensions or three-dimensional visualisations are not used. Upgrades to new and improved CAD software may also increase the hardware specification required. Laptops used for work on site should incorporate a good colour screen and a large hard drive.

Monitors should be free from distortion and be the largest affordable. Larger screens make it easier to see larger images and to deal with small details.

Plotters produce their output with either pens, an electrostatic charge, or ink jets. Large plotters make it possible to output very large drawings, although bureau services are available if large drawings are rarely needed. Good ink jet or laser printers and colour ink jet plotters can produce excellent drawings in small sizes at modest prices.

Scanners and digitisers vary in size and in terms of the resolution at which they can process an image. Typical desktop scanners operate at a resolution of around 360 dots-per-inch (dpi) which may be adequate for most purposes. However, it may be desirable to scan an image at a higher resolution if it contains complex detail which is later to be vectorised. Similarly, large tablets or drum scanners make it easier to scan large maps or plans. In both cases it is important to check that the digitiser will offer the required output and it may be advantageous to hire bureau services rather than purchasing expensive equipment.

4.3 CAD LAYERS, NAMING CONVENTIONS AND DRAWING COLOURS

As the model is constructed, various portions of the model are placed on different layers (see Section 2.3). The layers should be designed to distinguish material in the model according to important criteria, for example, building part, building phase, site stratum, material, chronological standing, etc. Each layer should hold only a portion of the model as putting too much on a single layer may cause problems when the model is used for analysis. Objects can be moved from layer to layer, but this is harder to handle if many objects are held on a single layer. More importantly, the way that the model is segmented will affect its usefulness.

Using different layers requires some system for assigning portions of the model to particular layers and a naming convention for those layers. For example, a model of an historic structure may have many layers – for phases, materials, functions, designer/builder, and so on. Potentially all models can be segmented in any number of ways. The scheme chosen should make it possible to find material according to multiple criteria and in this way the layering scheme permits users to access the layers very much as they might access parts of a database.

A shortcoming of the layering systems in CAD software is that there is no facility for creating a hierarchical scheme to match hierarchical recording systems. For example, a surveyor may record the ridge board, rafters and truss beams as separate components that taken together comprise the roof of a building. This is a hierarchical system but CAD software does not allow one layer to contain other layers, thus it may be difficult to re-group the separate roof components. One way of working around this shortcoming is to use the layer or file naming conventions to create relationships between components, e.g. all names beginning with A form a set which comprises AA, AB, AC etc.

4.3.1 Naming conventions for CAD layers

It is important to adopt a systematic approach to naming layers in CAD models. CAD systems permit searches based on layer names and some systems permit searches using 'wild-cards' which enable retrieval of sets of layers with structured names. In complex CAD models or models comprising cross-referenced files, it is important to be able to bring together layers without causing confusions through inappropriate use of layer names. For example, users often begin with layer names like *wall* and *door*, then graduate to *wall1* and *door1*. As the model grows, layer names grow longer, more complicated and harder to remember. Layers cannot easily be selected from the model according to their characteristics; instead a user must know all of the layer names and type in a subset when trying to select specific portions of a model. Even then it is difficult to be sure that all the relevant layers have been accessed.

The layer-naming scheme should be designed and specified as early in the project as possible. As the model grows, the use of the scheme will become more and more important. In deciding upon a layer-naming scheme, CAD users have the option of either adopting an existing convention or developing their own system. In either case it is important to make sure that the naming convention is documented, can be consistently applied and allows some flexibility for modification as the model develops.

The CSA layer-naming convention is an example of an existing scheme. It is a systematic naming convention that is based on layer names designed to specify the contents of each layer. Each character in the layer name designates information according to its position as well as by the letter itself (see Appendix 2). The CSA convention is a conceptual scheme that permits the layers of any CAD model to be accessed according to logical analytic categories that are meaningful and useful for a specific project. It is more general and more adaptable than a discipline-specific scheme, but works well only with programs that permit 'wild-card' searches for layers.

Some organisations define layer-naming conventions that are designed to meet specific, practical needs, for example architects might define conventions to be used by different professionals working on a development. English Heritage (English Heritage, 2000) has developed a systematic layer-naming convention for buildings archaeology, photogrammetric recording and topographic survey. This system accommodates CAD layers produced by other professions and has some of the features of the CSA system but with a more prescriptive list of layers (see Appendix 3).

Both the CSA and the English Heritage conventions have enough flexibility to be modified for specific projects. As a general rule any such changes should be systematically implemented throughout the model. With a complex scheme such as the CSA convention, the original model and layer-name models should be backed up and saved and checked once the new system has been established.

Documenting the layer-naming scheme is critical to a CAD project. Such documentation should include a list of the layer names or codes with a description of each. A description of how the layer-naming scheme has been developed and how it is applied is also useful, especially with a complex scheme. One method of tying the layer-naming convention to the CAD file is actually to include the scheme as a layer within the model.

4.3.2 Conventions for selecting drawing colours

It may seem that colours should be used like layers, to specify analytic aspects of a model. For example, a specific colour might be assigned to a given structure, or to a given stratum in an archaeological site. This can be done, but different colours should not be assigned to objects on the same layer of a drawing. The objects should be placed on appropriate layers first and then a colour should be assigned to each layer. All entities on a given layer will then be the same colour. The visual result may be the same, but the process is different because the layers, not the colours, hold the analytical distinctions.

There are two reasons to resist the temptation to use colours, rather than layers, to hold meaning:

* It is easier to change colours than to change layers and inadvertent colour changes could result in loss of meaning
* The print process generally uses colours or line weights in the model to determine the line colour or weight that is printed on paper. This means that the colours in the model may need to be changed every time a paper drawing is produced, since each tends to serve a particular purpose and emphasise different points.

The danger of losing important distinctions is too great if colours have been changed, and any distinctions between portions of the model should be made using layers.

4.4 INDICATING PRECISION ON DRAWINGS AND IN CAD

Precision is indicated on drawings through the use of significant digits (see sub-section 3.2.1). Where dimensions are shown, precision is clear. When dimensions are not shown on a drawing, they can be retrieved by making measurements on the drawing and, where appropriate, applying the scale factor. In such cases, the scale of the drawing is a limiting factor, and precision is limited by the double problem of scale – the accuracy with which the draughtsperson, working at reduced scale, can produce a line of appropriate length and the accuracy with which a user can measure and scale up a line on the drawing.

CAD models present a different problem for determining precision. All points are specified in a three-dimensional Cartesian grid system, and dimensions are calculated from those point locations. The precision of the point locations depends on the CAD system used but is the same for all points in any given model with trailing zeros being added or additional digits truncated. In most CAD systems, users may decide on the number of decimal places to be displayed. However, all point locations and dimensions must have the same number and will appear to have the same precision. Thus the number of decimal places displayed in a CAD model does not reflect the actual precision of any specific measurement and false precision may be suggested.

4.4.1 Mixed levels of precision

A model may contain very precise measurements alongside less precise ones because combined data capture techniques have been used. For example, a total station may be used along with steel tape measures to capture certain dimensions and, while the survey data may be accurate to the nearest millimetre, other data may have a 1cm tolerance (see Section 3.2). Separate CAD layers or cross-referenced drawings may be used to hold items with different levels of precision.

Levels of precision must be documented so that users of the model have ways to determine which measurements or locations have been more or less precisely determined. With this information the model can be used to extract additional measurements whose precision is known. The precision of any measurements can be no better than that of the reference points, but the situation is more complex still, since measurements taken from a single reference point may be very precise when compared with one another but not when compared with other points in the model. Careful documentation allows users to avoid the practice of using points from lower-tolerance data sources as reference points and also allows users to know when to expect good high-precision measurements.

4.4.2 Documenting precision

Since CAD systems cannot display differing levels of precision and may indicate spurious levels of precision, CAD models must be documented (see Sections 5.4, 5.5 and 5.6). This documentation should explain how precisely the dimensions and data points were determined, and how users can discriminate between more and less precise measurements if both are present. For example, different layers might be used for different levels of precision. The setting for displaying decimal places, if set within the model rather than the CAD program, should be appropriate to the precision used in measuring.

4.5 CAD DATA FORMATS

There is no standard format for exchanging CAD data between different software packages and the best advice on the subject comes from Lyman and Besser (1998) who suggest that CAD users should 'save in the most common file formats, [as] the more files that exist in a given format, the more likely that file converters or emulators will be written for that format (because of economies of scale).' At present the most commonly used CAD software is AutoCAD, made by AutoDesk; consequently it is recommended that CAD files are saved as both .dwg and .dxf. These formats are, however, not without their problems.

The most widely used CAD file format is .dwg, which is the proprietary format used by AutoCAD. Due to AutoCAD's market prominence, .dwg has become dominant and other software manufacturers have implemented Autodesk software to permit their users to read and/ or write .dwg files. Unfortunately this is not always effective, as incompatibilities between programs can create problems with data transfers. There are even problems of incompatibility between slightly different, although equally current, packages from the same software house. For example, AutoCAD MAP, made by Autodesk, supports additional data elements which will not be recognised by the basic AutoCAD package.

The OpenDWG Alliance has been formed with the aim of making the .dwg format into a public standard. The Alliance will parse the .dwg format, maintain information on it and supply its members with software to read and write .dwg files. Although software incompatibility may ultimately frustrate this work, there is a possibility that the OpenDWG Alliance will succeed in making .dwg a public standard.

Drawing exchange format (.dxf) is another proprietary standard developed by Autodesk as an output format to allow users to exchange AutoCAD data and to transfer files into other drawing programs. The .dxf format is very widely used but it is not controlled by a standards body and Autodesk can alter the format at will. There are also incompatibility problems with .dxf and in particular the problem that software packages which do not support particular versions of .dxf may still import the data but incompletely. Thus users may be unaware of the fact that data have been lost in the migration.

Another CAD file format which may be used for dissemination is Drawing Web format (.dwf). The .dwf is a highly compressed file that is created from a .dwg file and is used purely for publication on the Web. It is not recommended that CAD files are either stored or archived as .dwf.

Given the problems of incompatibilities between different file formats, and even incompatibilities between the same file format from the same manufacturer, it is recommended that CAD files are saved in the latest possible version of .dwg and .dxf, and that this is fully documented (see Section 5). CAD files will consequently require active digital curation and will need to be continually migrated to new versions of .dwf/.dwg as they are brought into use (see sub-section 6.5.2). After every migration it is necessary to check the files to ensure that there has been no loss of information during the migration process. Given their somewhat problematic nature, CAD files and documentation should be passed to an appropriate digital archive at the earliest opportunity (see Section 7).

Section 5: Documenting data from CAD projects

5.1 WHY DOCUMENT YOUR DATA?

Those working with CAD will be very familiar with its wide range of different uses. CAD software may be used to design something new or to record existing objects and structures. CAD projects differ widely and so do their outputs, which can range from very complex three-dimensional models to simple two-dimensional drawings. Projects may involve using CAD software to capture models which are transferred into GIS, to form the basis of virtual reality models or simply to create illustrations that are incorporated into reports and other publications.

While work is underway, it is relatively easy to remember the steps that have been taken to produce a model. After a short time has passed it becomes more difficult to remember how data were produced or compiled from different sources. It is helpful to prepare documentation as CAD projects proceed, recording the process by which models were created. The documentation produced will help both the project team and others in the future to assess the fitness of a model and datasets for use in particular purposes. This documentation will also form a vital component of the digital archive from a CAD project.

Depositing data in an archive is often the final stage of a project. Depositing data is important, not only to ensure preservation but also because it prompts the necessary attention to documentation throughout the project. The benefit is that once the data and its supporting documentation have been deposited the information contained therein can be made available for years to come.

5.1.1 LEVELS OF DOCUMENTATION

Documenting a large project that has produced thousands of CAD files may seem daunting. However, each individual CAD file does not necessarily require individual documentation containing thousands of pieces of information. To do so would be prohibitively expensive in terms of time and effort and would probably be unnecessary. Instead the amount of documentation can be minimised if it is produced in layers which relate to stages of the overall project. For example:

- Overall project description
- Methods and conventions of data capture
- Individual model documentation.

This system avoids duplication of information, so that details about the project, sources and the methods of data capture can be recorded once and then cross-referenced from the individual file documentation. Documentation at the individual file level can also be minimised if project managers decide to adopt standard layer-naming and other conventions at the outset of the project and there are no cross-reference files or attached databases. What is important is that the more detailed information is available within the documentation hierarchy, and that it can be easily located.

5.2 DOCUMENTATION FOR PROJECTS

It is important to plan the creation of digital data from the outset of a project. Projects generally begin with the preparation of a project design and it is at this stage that the tasks that are necessary to complete the intended work are planned and resources are allocated. At the design stage, it is recommended practice for project managers to define areas of responsibility for creating digital data including personnel, the acceptable file formats and naming conventions, as well as to identify both back-up and archiving strategies. Project managers are recommended to contact a digital archive at the design stage to check their recommended file formats, documentation requirements or any conditions of deposit so that these can be included in the planning process.

The project design itself forms a part of the project documentation, providing the background to why work took place and why CAD was used. The final report, written after the project's completion, should then describe the project outcomes, how the work was actually done and what was produced. Both documents describe the formats of data that were produced and factors which influenced their collection and later re-use. Both documents should be deposited as part of the project's digital archive.

5.2.1 Project level documention

Project level documentation provides summary information about the project for others. This information is often used to provide an index for resource discovery (see Section 6.6) to support the retrieval of project reports and associated data files. The following information should be collected:

Project name	The project name or title may be the name that is used in the written report (e.g 'The Athens Propylaea project') or a familiar/ published place or monument name (e.g. 'Symon's Castle').
Reference number	The project reference number or code used by the organisation responsible to refer to the project or to the data.
Project purpose	A brief summary (200–300 words) of the main aims and objectives of the project including a description of the work flow, data collection processes, personnel, with specific notes regarding successful or problematic portions of the work
Project keywords	Keywords indexing the subject of the project. They can be drawn from the index fields listed below (e.g. survey type, capture method,

	monument type, etc.) with reference to appropriate terminology standards (see Appendix 4).
Subject/Monument type	A brief description of the subject being recorded, i.e. the monument or structure surveyed. Use of the Thesaurus of Monument Types (RCHME 1995) is recommended to achieve consistency in terminology (see also Appendix 4).
Site address	The postal address of the subject being recorded (if any).
Administrative area	In the United Kingdom record the District/County/Unitary Authority in which the subject lies (in the United States this record will be the Town/County/State). The administrative boundaries that are current at the time of the survey should be used and, for consistency, the use of the standard names from Appendix 4 is recommended.
Country	The country in which the study area lies (England, Scotland and Wales should be recorded separately).
Spatial coverage	The map coordinates of the SW and NE corner of a bounding box enclosing the study area. For Britain, Ordnance Survey National Grid coordinates are recommended. It should be noted that the Ordnance Survey of Great Britain (OS) holds copyright over the reproduction of OS maps and retains Intellectual Property Rights in all information derived from such maps.
Size	The size of the study area.
Duration	The dates when the project took place, i.e. the dates of the first and last day on which the fieldwork took place. If separate periods of fieldwork are related to the same project they should be listed individually.
Originator	The name, address and role of the organisation or individual(s) responsible for the project.
Client	The name and address of the organisation or individual(s) who sponsored or commissioned the project.
Depositor	The name, address and role of the organisation or individual(s) depositing data from the project.
Primary archive	The name, address and role of the organisation or individual(s) holding primary data from the project.
Related archives	References to the original material for any data derived in whole or in part from published or unpublished sources, whether printed or machine-readable. Details should be given of where the sources are held and how they are identified there (e.g. by accession number). If a CAD model is derived from other sources it should be indicated whether the data represent a complete or partial transcription/copy, and the methodology used for their computerisation.
Bibliography	The title, author, date and publisher of any report(s) or publication(s) about the project
Copyright	A description of any known copyrights associated with the digital collection.

5.3 DOCUMENTING THE CONVENTIONS

CAD projects often involve bringing together datasets captured both in the field and at the desk-top. Several different people may be involved in the project in different roles at different times (e.g. surveyors, digitisation operators, CAD operators etc.). The data that they capture may be brought together as separate layers within a CAD model or as cross-referenced files. For instance, a CAD model may include both field survey data and data that have been digitised from maps, plans and photographs.

It is recommended practice for project managers to agree standard layer-naming (see Section 4.3) and file-naming conventions at the start of the project. These conventions facilitate the process of both data capture and in building CAD models.

5.3.1 Project layer-naming convention

Documentation should be provided for the layer-naming convention that has been adopted for the project. This should include:

Name of convention   The name of the layer-naming convention; this may be an agreed standard convention used by an organisation (e.g. the English Heritage layer-naming convention, see Appendix 3) or a local convention agreed for a specific project. Full details of the layer name, content and drawing conventions should be documented unless details have been published, in which case it may be sufficient to provide a publication reference.

Repeat this information for each layer used:

Layer name   The name or code associated with the layer (e.g. OA-ROOF is the layer name associated with all roof timbers in the English Heritage convention).

Layer content   A brief description of the content of the layer (e.g. roof timbers).

Drawing conventions   Drawing conventions or any special icons and characters used in this layer.
- Font type
- Line type
- Drawing element
- Colour

5.3.2 Project file-naming convention

Many organisations and individuals use file-naming conventions, which are used to identify details such as the project to which the file relates, its content, the version number and format. When depositing data in an archive it is helpful to provide documentation for these conventions. The information recorded should include:

File names   It is important to choose meaningful file names and to provide a brief explanation of any abbreviations used. For example, 'GPS survey files start with a 'g' and are then indexed with a subsequent number: g1, g2...' etc.

File extensions	It is recommended that standard file extensions are used to reflect the format of the data contained in the file, e.g., .dwg, .txt.
File formats	Provide an explanation of which internal format is associated with a particular file extension, e.g. which version of .dwg or .dxf file format has been used.

5.4 DOCUMENTING FIELD DATA CAPTURE

Those involved in the survey will generally begin recording information about data as soon as they begin to create or use it. **Log books** are often used to record information as the project proceeds. It is normal to record details of the equipment and software used, any problems that were encountered or modifications that were made to standard procedures or naming conventions.

   Some information about each on-site survey technique used is required. This helps to assess the suitability of the archived results for later use in a CAD model. Such information would enable the precision and accuracy of the data to be assessed to determine, for example, if it was suitable for use in producing a three-dimensional model.

   The following is a list of the forms of documentation that might be useful to record for each survey technique:

Project name	Include the project name or title with the documentation to cross-refer to the project level documentation.
Reference number	Include the project reference number (if any) with the documentation to cross-refer to the project level documentation.
Survey type	The type of survey technique should be recorded, e.g. total station survey, GPS survey, direct object scanning, hand measurement survey etc.
Survey purpose	Provide a brief summary (200–300 words) describing the survey, the techniques used, including training procedures, and equipment checks as appropriate.
Duration	The dates when the survey took place, i.e. the dates of the first and last day of the survey. If separate pieces of fieldwork took place they should be listed separately.
Surveyor	The name and address of the organisation or individual(s) who carried out the survey.
Survey keywords	Keywords indexing the type of survey technique.
Instrumentation	Specific information about the make and model of the instruments used and their test and repair records as appropriate.
Coverage	Describe the area covered and the methods used (e.g. fixed grid) for each technique.
Precision and accuracy	This should provide a commentary on the accuracy and precision of the data captured by a particular technique. This might include: • The estimated error of survey base station coordinates • Data precision

- Data accuracy
- Data density
- The estimated error terms for the coordinate pairs and (if appropriate) the z-coordinate
- Georeferencing information.

Data transfer files   The data transfer files (if any) used to move survey data from a total station to a computer and any intermediate files used in that process. Record the following information:
- File name
- Date
- A summary of the work done
- Data points + numbers, etc.

5.4.1 Additional information for GPS data

In addition, the following information is recommended for data captured using GPS equipment:

Location method   Record the method that was used to locate stations, C/A or P code pseudorange measurements, carrier phase measurements and whether a single measurement or averaging (include the time period) was used.

Coordinate transformation   Record the software used for any coordinate transformation and give the associated error estimates.

Satellite   The satellites used in obtaining fix and observed GDOP (Geometric Dilution of Precision, a measure of the quality of the fix indicating the suitability of satellite positions for triangulation).

Differential correction   The nature of any differential correction undertaken together with error estimates

Broadcast   The broadcast differential: name of the service provider and the name and location of base station

Base station   The local base station: instrument details, location (including error estimate) of base station

Post-processing   Post-processing software used and the source of correction data.

5.4.2 Notes and hand measurements

Most forms of survey involve taking notes and making annotated drawings as part of the process. Much survey work also involves some hand measurements with tapes and line levels, even if the major part of the work is done using electronic equipment. For example, hand measurements may be used in inaccessible areas while fixed points are surveyed with electronic equipment to specify the relationships between the different areas of the site.

Notes and drawings form part of the project archive, although not part of the digital archive unless they are retrospectively digitised. They include:

- Drawings of the survey subject with markers showing the data points
- Specifying data points with three coordinates for three-dimensional models

- Date produced
- Name of the originator.

5.5 DOCUMENTING OFF-SITE DATA CAPTURE

5.5.1 Sources of data

Numerous sources are used to capture data retrospectively into CAD models, including survey plans, Ordnance Survey and other maps, aerial photographs or ground photographs. Each of these sources is of value for a different purpose and each brings with it a different set of problems. For example, data acquired at 1:50,000 scale may be ideally suited for plotting a distribution map but is unsuited for recording the location of individual excavation trenches.

Ownership of data may well prove quite complex. For example, data originating from the Ordnance Survey may be used by North Yorkshire County Council to derive a new dataset 'owned' by the County Council. These data may in turn be used by York Archaeological Trust to derive a further new dataset. Although little of the original resource may survive, the Ordnance Survey continues to hold intellectual property rights which must be recognised and which may well affect later uses of the data, e.g. publication on the Internet.

To support future uses of project data that have been captured by desk-top techniques it is important to record information both about the original source and the digitisation process. The following information should be recorded for each data source that is digitised:

Project name	Include the project name or title with the documentation to cross-refer to the project level documentation.
Reference number	Include the project reference number (if any) with the documentation to cross-refer to the project level documentation.
Source name	Record the name of the original source, e.g. map and the map series.
Source reference	Record the reference number for the source, if any.
Type of source	Keyword indexing the general type of the source material, e.g. map, plan, photograph, drawing.
Source medium	Keyword describing the medium of the source, i.e. paper, mylar, acetate.
Publisher	The name and address of the publisher of the original source, if any.
Copyright	A description of any known copyrights held on the source material including details of the permitted uses of copyright data, e.g. an organisation may have copyright clearance to use a map in a CAD model and publish an illustration incorporating map details in the project report but not to publish the same illustration on the Internet.
Scale	Scale of the original source, given as a ratio, and the original scale (where the source is an enlargement or generalisation from another source).
Accuracy	Claimed accuracy of the source.

Additional information for maps

In addition to the information listed above, the following details are recommended:

Accuracy Claimed accuracy for any specific components: map makers will often provide an estimated precision for contour lines or other sub-components of a map.

Map projection All details of the map projection and coordinate system employed. This information is usually printed on the mapsheet or else should be sought from the map source.

Additional information for photographs

In addition to the information listed above the following details are recommended:

Photographic details Full photographic details including camera position, focal length, distance from object/flying height (for vertical aerial photographs) etc.

Ground control Details regarding the ground control points (GCPs) used in georeferencing.

5.5.2 Documenting retrospective data capture

Techniques The generic category of conversion technique used, e.g. digitising, scanning etc.

Equipment The make and model of hardware device used, e.g. scanner.

Software Software driver and version used.

Parameters The parameters of the device, e.g. scan resolution, no. of bits per pixel or line precision.

Post-processing Details of any post-processing on the data, e.g. noise reduction.

Automatic processing Details of any automatic vector processing applied to the theme (such as snap-to-nearest-node).

Control points Details of control points used to manage conversion from digitiser.

Data precision and accuracy Brief assessment of the precision and accuracy or any errors that occurred during automatic vectorisation processes.

Copyright A description of any known copyrights held in the digitised material including details of the permitted uses of copyright data.

Data files
- File name
- Date
- A summary of the work done
- Data-points, numbers, etc.

5.6 DOCUMENTING CAD MODELS

Each project may produce a number of CAD models. Where standard file and layer-naming conventions are used these will be documented as part of the overall project metadata (see Section 5.3), which can be cross-referred to in this documentation. If new or modified layer-naming conventions are used in the creation of the model, these must be documented at this stage.

5.6.1 List of all files

For each project provide a list of all files that have been produced including:

- File name
- Create date or date of last update
- Copyright
- Data format of the file, i.e. the version number
- Description of content.

It is important to record all known copyright details in each file. In cases where data has been retrospectively captured from another source (such as a map or photograph) there may be a complex trail of ownership of copyright. It makes life easier for everyone if the process of evolution is recorded, particularly as copyright permissions may be limited for some datasets (e.g. it may be permissible to use a map for research but not for publication). When preparing a CAD model for deposit in a digital archive, it is recommended practice to link any copyright-restricted datasets as external reference files rather than embedding them within a CAD model.

5.6.2 Documentation for each CAD model

For each model the documentation should include:

Project name	Include the project name or title with the documentation to cross-refer to the project level documentation.
Reference number	Include the project reference number (if any) with the documentation to cross-refer to the project level documentation.
Creator	Record the name and address of the organisation or individual(s) responsible for creating the CAD model.
Name of CAD model	The name of the CAD model, which will often be the name of the site.
CAD software	The type and version number of the CAD software used, e.g. AutoCad release 10. Give details of any updates or revisions to the software and portions of the model associated with each version.
Files used	Provide a list of files used in the model. For cross-referenced files the full file name with directory path must be recorded.
Layer convention	Note the name of the layer-naming convention used by the project and document any amendments made to this convention in the model, including changes to line type, colour, drawing elements etc.

5.6.3 Documentation for any attached external database

Project name	Include the project name or title with the documentation to cross-refer to the project level documentation.

Project reference   Include the project reference number (if any) with the documentation to cross-refer to the project level documentation.

Database   Type and version number of database used, e.g. MS Access version 2.0.

Name   The name of the database, data table or data file. This would incorporate the project reference number.

Data field   For each data field:
- field name
- any codes used
- description, if coded data is used a complete list of any codes with a description of each code should be provided.

CAD file   The name of the CAD file with which the database is linked.

Link field   Name of the linking field between the database and CAD model.

File format   The format in which the database has been saved.

Creation date   The date when the database was created.

Back-up files that are created while work is in progress should be stored separately, in case there is any need to restore the CAD model from a back-up during the life of the project (see Section 6.4).

5.7 DOCUMENTATION CASE STUDY: SYMON'S CASTLE
BY JEREMY HUGGETT

Symon's Castle is a 13th century AD timber and earthwork castle situated on the Welsh borders (see also Section 2.9). It was excavated in a series of one-month seasons from 1985 to 1994 by Dr Jeremy Huggett (University of Glasgow) and Dr Chris Arnold (then of University of Wales Aberystwyth) as a research and training excavation. The castle consists of two platforms separated by a ditch; the whole of the north-east platform (the 'bailey') was excavated, a section through the ditch, and the whole of the interior of the south-west platform (the 'motte') with sections through the stone-revetted clay bank on its perimeter.

As a result of the degraded nature of the soil, few archaeological contexts could be defined on any basis other than the relative density, distribution and nature of stone and artefacts alone. In the absence of distinct layers of soil over much of the excavated area, the removal of the deposits was carried out in a series of arbitrary spits. Individual context numbers were only assigned where layers and features were clearly defined (usually as a result of burning). Hence the recording of all non-artefactual material comprised a series of drawings on which the objective data were all stones larger than about 0.03m in their greatest dimension, with any apparent 'edges' in stones or soil highlighted. For any given area this record comprised a maximum of four drawings: Plan 1: the visible and normally amorphous surface following the removal of the vegetation; Plan 2: the pattern revealed following the removal of topsoil; Plan 3: the distribution of stones lying directly on the subsoil or bedrock; and Plan 4: any stones which appeared to have been set into the subsoil by human agency. All artefacts, including burnt clay and charcoal fragments, were recorded in three dimensions, and the importance of this for the subsequent identification of structures that had no earth-fast timbers is demonstrated in Section 2.9.

Digitisation of the plan data was carried out as part of the post-excavation phase. In the absence of a large-format scanner (although a bureau service could have been used), all the original A1 (approx.) field plans in pencil on permatrace were scanned in overlapping sections using an A3 scanner. To create stone plans, the scans were sharpened and converted to 2-bit black and white images which were automatically traced. These traces were subsequently imported, scaled, rotated and positioned on the site grid in AutoCAD 2000, along with the original grey-scale scans. The overlaps between traces were removed and the plans cleaned manually with reference to the underlying scanned images. To create individual context plans, the extents of contexts were manually digitised from the scaled and rotated and positioned grey-scale scans. A series of interpretative three-dimensional models were constructed on the basis of the excavated evidence (see Huggett and Chen 2000). An intra-site GIS was also constructed for analysis by importing the digitised stone and context plans, which had been saved in AutoCAD version 14 format for compatibility, into IDRISI and ArcView version 3.2.

The digital archive created by the Symon's Castle project is a research level archive and includes:

- Project reports covering the stratigraphic sequence
- CAD files
- Layer-naming convention.

5.7.1 Project documentation

Project name	Symon's Castle project.
Reference number	None.
Project purpose	Excavation of a 13th century AD timber and earthwork castle near Churchstoke, Powys. The project was directed by Dr C. Arnold and Dr J. Huggett over a 10 year period, on site for four weeks per year. The excavation was run as a training school for university students and other interested parties, and as a volunteer excavation. Although the site was largely undisturbed, the soil was very shallow and highly leached, requiring a modified recording procedure and full three-dimensional recording of artefacts.
Project keywords	Excavation, Medieval, castle, motte and bailey, timber and earthwork.
Subject	Timber and earthwork castle, with stone-revetted clay rampart and timber palisades, timber buildings in interior.
Site address	Symon's Castle, Churchstoke, Powys.
Administrative area	Churchstoke, Powys
Country	Wales.
Spatial coverage	(OSGB) SO 285 933
Size	Not reported.
Duration	1985–1994.
Originator	Dr J. Huggett, Department of Archaeology, University of Glasgow, Dr C. Arnold.
Client	None.

Bibliography	J. Huggett and C. Arnold (1998) Symon's Castle (http://www.gla.ac.uk/archaeology/projects/symon/)
	C. Arnold and J. Huggett (in prep), Symon's Castle, Churchstoke, Powys: Excavations 1985–1994.
	J. Huggett and Chen Guo-Yuan (2000) '3-D Interpretative Modelling of Archaeological Sites: A Computer Reconstruction of a Medieval Timber and Earthwork Castle' *Internet Archaeology* 8, (http://intarch.ac.uk/journal/issue8/huggett_index.html")
Copyright	Dr J. Huggett and Dr C. Arnold

5.7.2 Layer-naming convention

The project defined three layer-naming conventions, for the stone plans, the context plans and for three-dimensional models. Each convention is described below, with AutoCAD Colour Index (ACI) being used to define the colours used.

Convention:	**Stone plans**
Layer name	**Description**
Bedrock	Layer content: Extent of exposed bedrock Source: Project files Colour: Green (AutoCAD Colour Index 100) Line type: Continuous
Exc_edge	Layer content: Edge of excavation Source: Project files Colour: Magenta (ACI 211) Line type: Continuous
Scan	Layer content: Links to original scanned images of stone plans Source: Project files Colour: Grey-green (ACI 54) Line type: Continuous
aXbY	Layer content: Stone plan where a = area of site (m=motte, b=bailey, t=terrace, d=ditch); X = plan level (1, 2, 3 etc.), b = sheet of plan X, Y = scanned element of sheet b Source: Project files Colour: White (ACI 249) Line type: Continuous

Convention:	**Context plans**
Layer name	**Description**
Bedrock	Layer content: Extent of exposed bedrock Source: Project files Colour: Green (ACI 100) Line type: Continuous
Exc_edge	Layer content: Edge of excavation Source: Project files

	Colour: Magenta (ACI 211)
	Line type: Continuous
Context X	Layer content: Context extent.
(X = context number)	Source: Project files
	Colour: Red (ACI 240)
	Line type: Continuous

Convention	**Three dimensional models**
Layer name	**Description**
Topography	Layer content: Surface mesh of topographic survey
	Source: Project files
	Colour: Green (ACI 84)
	Line type: Continuous
Palisade	Layer content: Palisade posts
	Source: Project files
	Colour: Brown (ACI 14)
	Line type: Continuous
Planktimber	Layer content: Palisade planking
	Source: Project files
	Colour: Yellow (ACI 50)
	Line type: Continuous
Road	Layer content: Roadway on bailey to bridge
	Source: Project files
	Colour: Mustard (ACI 52)
	Line type: Continuous
Bridge	Layer content: Bridge between motte and bailey
	Source: Project files
	Colour: Gold (ACI 40)
	Line type: Continuous

5.7.3 File-naming convention

Each stone plan file is named by its area and plan level – hence Motte Plan 1, Motte Plan 2, Bailey Plan 1, etc. and standard file extensions. Each individual context plan file is named using the site context number and standard file extensions, e.g. 12345.dwg.

5.7.4 On-site data capture documentation

Project name	Symon's Castle
Reference number	None
Survey type	**Planning**
Survey purpose	Standard site planning on permatrace, employing 1m square drawing frames and hand tapes. All plans drawn to a scale of 1:20.
Duration	1985–1994 (approx. 10 months in total)
Surveyor	Dr J. Huggett and Dr C. Arnold
Survey keywords	Hand measurement, level

Instrumentation	Level
Coverage	Entire excavated area
Precision and accuracy	Measurements to nearest centimetre, estimated accuracy ±5cm
Data transfer files	N/A
Project name	Symon's Castle
Reference number	None
Survey type	**Topographic survey**
Survey purpose	Approx. 5000 spot heights measured across area of site at 1m intervals. Grid reconstructed in local areas using tapes anchored by permanent steel pins.
Duration	1985–1986 (approx. 2 weeks in total)
Surveyor	Dr J. Huggett and Dr C. Arnold
Survey keywords	Hand measurement, level
Instrumentation	Level
Coverage	Entire area of earthworks
Precision and accuracy	Measurements to nearest centimetre, estimated accuracy ±10cm
Data transfer files	Symondem.img – IDRISI image format, heights in centimetres at one-metre intervals, 76 columns x 72 rows, 0 is null value
	Symon.asc – ASCII text format, heights in centimetres at one-metre intervals, 76 columns x 72 rows, 0 is null value.

5.7.5 Off-site data capture documentation

Project name	Symon's Castle
Reference number	N/A
Source name	**Plans (stones)**
Source reference	None
Type of source	Drawing
Source medium	Permatrace
Publisher	None
Copyright	Dr J. Huggett and Dr C. Arnold
Scale	1:20
Accuracy	±5cm (estimated)
Techniques	Scanning
Equipment	Scanner = Umax Mirage IISE
Software	MagicScan 4.2
Software	PaintShop Pro 6.0
Software	RasterVect 5.2
Parameters	Scanner maximum resolution = 9800 dpi x 9800 dpi; scan resolution = 150 dpi; filter used = sharpen
Post-processing	Outlines sharpened (Image/Sharpen/Sharpen more) if needed and converted to 2-bit black and white images (Colours/Decrease Colour Depth/2 Colours). Software used: PaintShop Pro 6.0
Automatic processing	Auto-traced using centrelines with arc and circle recognition turned off. Software used: RasterVect 5.2

Control points	Site grid fixed points on plans.
Data precision and accuracy	Tracing precision: 1.5 pixels, minimal length of line: 1 pixel. Resulting plans cleaned manually, though polylines representing the smallest stones (*c.* 5cm or less) were not closed.
Data files	AutoCAD dxf/dwg, version 14

Project name	Symon's Castle
Reference number	N/A
Source name	**Plans (contexts)**
Source reference	None
Type of source	Drawing
Source medium	Permatrace
Publisher	None
Copyright	Dr J. Huggett and Dr C. Arnold
Scale	1:20
Accuracy	±5cm (estimated)
Techniques	Digitising
Equipment	Digitising tablet = A3 Summagraphics Summasketch III
Software	AutoCAD 2000
Parameters	Tablet claimed accuracy ±0.010 inches; resolution: 2540 lines per inch.
Post-processing	N/A
Automatic processing	N/A
Control points	Site grid fixed points on plans
Data precision and accuracy	Not given
Data files	AutoCAD dwg, version 14

5.7.6 List of all files

File name	Date	Copyright	Format	Content
Motte Plan 1.dwg	12/08/2001	JWH/CJA	dwg version 14	Motte stone plan at Plan 1 stage
Motte Plan 2.dwg	12/08/2001	JWH/CJA	dwg version 14	Motte stone plan at Plan 2 stage
...				
41.dwg	20/01/2002	JWH/CJA	dwg version 14	Extent of context 41
42.dwg	20/01/2002	JWH/CJA	dwg version 14	Extent of context 42

N.B. These details would be repeated for each file in the archive.

5.7.7 Documenting the CAD models

Project name	Symon's Castle
Project reference number	None
Name of CAD model	Interpretative reconstruction

Creator	Chen Guo-Yuan and J. Huggett
CAD software	AutoCAD 14
Files used	Sym_22.dwg (topographic surface)
	Hall_1.dwg (version 1 of the hall)
	Tower_2.dwg (version 2 of the tower)
	Symlisp.lsp (AutoLISP programs for construction of timber palisades, wallwalks, roadway and bridge)
Layer convention	3D models layer convention with additional layers as follows:-
	Hallrftimber: Colour = brown (ACI 33); Line type = continuous (rooftimbers of hall)
	Hallroof: Colour = gold (ACI 41); Line type = continuous (roof of hall)
	Hallwall: Colour = red (ACI 10); Line type = continuous (walls of hall)
	Hallwindow: Colour = maroon (ACI 242); Line type = continuous (windows/doorway of hall)
	Towerroof: Colour = gold (ACI 41); Line type = continuous (roof of tower)
	Towerstair: Colour = orange (ACI 30); Line type = continuous (stair within tower)
	Towertimber: Colour = brown (ACI 42); Line type = continuous (timber framework of tower)
	Towerwall: Colour = red/brown (ACI 12); Line type = continuous (planked walls of tower)

N.B. This documentation would be repeated for each model in the archive.

Section 6: Good practice in managing CAD models for digital archiving

6.1 INTRODUCTION

CAD models are created from data which are collected, manipulated and developed in a digital environment. This puts them in a special position with regard to archiving as the ever-increasing pace of change in computer hardware and software means that in a few years' time these precious research materials may be lost forever. The best strategy for long-term preservation of data in digital formats is for them to be systematically collected, maintained and made accessible to users operating in very different computing environments.

Digital archiving is different from traditional archiving. Traditional archiving practice seeks to preserve physical objects (e.g. artefacts, samples, paper, photographs, microfilm) that carry information. Digital archiving is about preserving information regardless of the media on which that information is stored. This is because diskettes and other magnetic and optical media degrade, and software and hardware change rapidly: therefore the physical media on which digital data are stored are impermanent.

For all practical purposes, data from any project will only continue to be available if the data have been archived. It is important to put archival storage plans in effect from the moment data gathering begins.

6.2 THE ARCHIVAL NEED

It is not obvious to all that digital data must receive special care. However, the problems that can arise were demonstrated in the United Kingdom through ADS work rescuing the contents of the Newham Museum Archaeological Service digital archive (Austin *et al.* 2001). The Archaeological Service was closed down in 1998 and its digital archive was passed to the ADS. This represented all the work they had digitised over a period of about ten years, and it was delivered to the ADS on 230 floppy disks containing over 6000 files. The data were largely in archaic formats or proprietary software and were inadequately documented. Significant time and effort was required in rescuing these files. Unfortunately, around 10–15% of the files are still inaccessible, including a series of site matrices that were produced in an early version of TurboCAD. These files can neither be converted into DXF nor read by modern versions of TurboCAD and thus the data that they contain are effectively lost.

Digital archives require special care for the following reasons:

- Magnetic and optical storage systems for digital data have finite lives and data files must be copied onto new storage media on a regular basis to prevent loss
- Digital data formats change rapidly, some becoming obsolete in a few years. A decade is a long period in the digital world. Data that are held in non-preservation file formats, i.e. proprietary file formats, can become irretrievable as versions of software packages go out of use
- Non-existent or inadequate documentation makes it difficult to reconstruct which data goes with which project and limits the potential for re-use.

The absence of a standard file format for CAD (see Section 4.5) is a particular problem. Although DXF is the most widely used format for CAD it is a proprietary standard developed by AutoDesk and has changed slightly with virtually every new release of AutoCAD.

The Newham Museum Service digital archive makes a salutary tale, but it is important to remember that it was compiled at a time when digital archiving was in its infancy. The purpose of this series of *Guides to Good Practice* is to put strategies and methodologies in place to ensure effective digital archiving of project data.

6.3 PLANNING FOR THE CREATION OF DIGITAL DATA

From the moment a project begins, careful thought must go into the preparation of the digital archive that will be delivered at the project's conclusion. Planning should include:

- **Preparing a project design** that documents the tasks necessary for the successful completion of the project at its outset, and includes a summary of the types of digital data that will be created. It is important to update this documentation throughout the life of the project (see Section 5.2)
- **Defining and documenting areas of responsibility** for creating and managing digital files at all stages of their life
- **Planning the file formats that will be used** for both the secure archiving and the dissemination of data. The formats used for these two activities may be different (see Section 4.5)
- **Checking** with the digital archive facility destined to receive the files **to see if there are any guidelines or standards that should be followed**. If local guidelines do not exist, it is recommended that the guidelines in this document are followed and that the ADS is consulted for up-to-date information (see Section 7.4).

6.3.1 Speed

Data, accompanied by adequate documentation, should be deposited in a digital archive as quickly as possible after the conclusion of the project. There are two reasons for this:

- Some kinds of digital degradation can occur quickly and prompt archiving is desirable
- Prompt archiving helps project personnel and archive staff to make sure that adequate documentation has been provided for long-term archival care of the files. If too much time passes before deposit, it may be difficult for project personnel to reconstruct the information required by the archive.

6.4 STORING DIGITAL DATASETS

During the working life of a project, digital data may be created on the hard disks of standalone PCs, on laptop computers or on network drives. Data may be acquired or stored on floppy disks, back-up tapes, CD-ROMs or other electronic media. Whatever the initial storage media, ideally digital files that are in use should be routinely backed up and this may involve transferring them onto a network drive.

Fireproof, anti-magnetic facilities are extremely important for the safe storage of digital media, and back-up versions should be stored separated from original media. Make sure that data documentation is included with the storage media. It is also important to make sure that there is a separate record of where the files are stored and how they are labelled.

6.4.1 File-naming conventions

Digital files should be given meaningful titles that reflect their content. Plan to use standard file-naming conventions and directory structures from the beginning of a project. If possible, use consistent conventions across all projects, for example:

- Reserve the 3-letter file extension for application specific codes, e.g. DWG, DXF, TIF
- Include some means of identifying the relevant activity in the file name, e.g. a unique reference number, project number or project name
- Include version number information in the file name where necessary.

Files created directly in DOS must use standard 8 character file names with 3 character file extensions. Longer and more meaningful file names are generally permitted under a Windows environment.

6.4.2 Version control

It is extremely important to maintain strict version control when working with files, especially with CAD models which may be processed using a series of different treatments.

There are three common strategies for providing version control: file-naming conventions, standard headers listing creation dates and version numbers, or file logs. It is important to record, where practical, every change to a file no matter how small the change. Versions that are no longer needed should be weeded out, after making sure that adequate back-up files have been created.

Another aid to version control is to use separate directories for raw, working and archive data. All primary field data (including the first loading in a CAD drawing) should be 'archived' as it comes in from the field and a copy taken as the 'working file' for editing. Then each identifiable product, for example, aggregations of single archaeological context drawings into group or phase drawings, can be archived separately. The key is to have separate folders for files in each directory to ensure that the data cannot be accidentally updated and overwritten. An index should be created for each directory.

6.4.3 Secure backing-up

Back-up is the familiar task of ensuring that there is an emergency copy, or a snap-shot, of data held somewhere else, in case of disaster. For a small project this may mean a single file held on a floppy disk or over a network; for a larger project or dataset it may mean complicated procedures of disaster planning, with fireproof cupboards, off-site copies and daily, weekly and monthly copies. These are important in the lifespan of the project but are not the same as long-term archiving of the data.

The **'Grandparent-Parent-Child' strategy** is the most widely used. The system works by rotating full and partial back-ups on each day of the week or month:

- The 'Parent' is the most recent full back-up and contains a snap-shot of the system at the start of a week
- 'Children' are normally daily back-ups containing only the changes to the system made on that day. These tapes are generally recycled every time a new Parent is created
- The 'Grandparent' is a complete snap-shot of the system that is taken every month. This should be stored in perpetuity and would not normally be recycled. This back-up can be brought out in moments of real crisis.

The system can be tailored to individual requirements; for a small dataset, or one that changes infrequently, such regular copying may be excessive and the time periods may be expanded or contracted as necessary. It is best practice that the weekly and monthly back-ups are stored away from the office, preferably in a secure, fireproof, anti-magnetic environment.

It is important to **validate** the back-up copies to ensure that all formatting and important data have been accurately preserved. Create back-ups when a project is complete or dormant, prior to any major changes, or if files are large enough to cause handling difficulties on the network. Each back-up should be clearly labelled, and its location should be logged.

6.4.4 Virus checking and other issues

Viruses are self-executing programs that enter a computing system hidden inside harmless programs or files, or disguised to encourage unsuspecting users to install them. Once in a system, they replicate themselves and carry out operations which range from the invisible to the vaguely irritating to the absolutely devastating. **Trojans** are programs that appear to have useful or desirable features that entice people to install or download them but they actually exist to do damage. Trojans do not replicate themselves and once the damage has been repaired they do not return. **Worms** are similar to viruses in that they replicate themselves and often interfere with the normal use of a computer or a program. Worms differ in that they exist as separate entities; they do not attach themselves to other files or programs.

While the damage that viruses, trojans and worms do can be great, the actual risk is less than some would believe. Experience suggests that much of the damage blamed on viruses and trojans is actually the effect of poor management. There is, however, a constant and real if minor risk from genuine, malicious programs which, because they are invisible, can come from the most innocent of sources.

There are some basic steps which can be taken to avoid viruses, trojans and worms:

- Install anti-virus software on the computer, and make sure that it is routinely upgraded (every month) because new viruses and trojans are constantly being designed and older software might not identify these

- Be suspicious of any unsolicited programs or files, particularly from unwanted email
- Don't download any more software from the Internet than is strictly necessary
- Scan all files received with the appropriate software, even those from a close colleague or friend.
- Don't forward emails called things like 'Virus Warning': most of these are hoaxes and some are viruses. Consult the lists maintained by anti-virus software houses before forwarding these messages
- When buying software, look for an anti-virus guarantee
- Have a back-up strategy in place should the worst happen.

6.5 DIGITAL ARCHIVING STRATEGIES

Digital archiving strategies do not, and should not, rely on the preservation of a single disk, tape, or CD-ROM. The essence of digital archiving lies in one of three strategies (Beagrie and Greenstein 1998):

- The first relies on migration of information from older hardware and software systems to newer systems, and **this is the strategy recommended for most archaeological applications**
- The second digital archiving strategy attempts the emulation of older hardware/software systems in newer systems. This is technically challenging, extremely expensive, and becomes increasingly difficult as current technology becomes ever more remote from the original systems employed. Emulation is consequently not recommended for archaeological archives
- The third digital archiving strategy is the complete preservation of old hardware and software systems. This costly high-risk strategy is not justifiable unless data cannot be migrated and are of substantial international importance.

Digital archiving in archaeology should revolve around a policy of controlled data migration. There are four main activities required for successful digital archiving with this strategy:
1   data refreshment
2   data migration
3   documentation
4   data management tools.

6.5.1 Data refreshment

Data refreshment is the act of copying information from one medium to the next as the original medium nears the end of its reliable lifespan. Research into the lifespan of both magnetic and optical media has been conducted. The overwhelming conclusion from this research is that, even though magnetic media can be safe for 5–10 years and optical media may survive more than 30, technology changes much more quickly. Digital media are far more likely to become unreadable as a result of changing technology than they are through media degradation. For example, 10 years ago many archaeologists collected information on 3-inch Amstrad diskettes. These diskettes are completely unreadable by PC machines, and cannot be accessed unless a surviving Amstrad is networked or has a peripheral such as a 3.5-inch disk drive connected though the serial port of the computer. Even then, as Amstrads use a different operating system to PCs, the data need to be exported in a standard format such as ASCII. On the other hand, if archaeologists had refreshed their data from 3-inch Amstrad diskettes to 5.25-inch disks and then to 3.5-inch disks, these digital data would still be accessible.

The architecture of hardware changes rapidly, but not as rapidly as software. Data created or gathered in a proprietary software format is hostage to the long-term viability of that brand, and the company that produces it. These cannot be assured. Certain types of file have been earmarked as industry standard formats, while in other cases there may be open formats available that, while losing some of the original versatility, may nonetheless allow reconstruction or importation into other updated software types.

6.5.2 Data migration

Data migration is even more important than data refreshment. Migration is the act of copying digital information from one format or structure into another (Wheatley 2001). One example is copying old flat-field database files into a newer relational database. The functionality of a flat-field database can be maintained in a relational database structure. In this case, migration also enables improvements in functionality as the data handling and retrieval capabilities of relational databases can be drawn upon.

Migration of data produced by CAD software is problematic because there is no standard format for exchange (see Section 4.5). Although CAD software allows data to be exported in DXF formats, each package creates DXF files differently. In practice this means that a CAD program may refuse to import a DXF file created in another program or it may import some sections of a file while omitting others without clear warning. The unwary can find that without careful migration much of the original information is lost when creating a new file.

In order for a digital archivist to migrate digital information successfully, it is necessary to understand the structure of the data fully, and how different parts relate to one another. It is important to retain the original media until the migrated data have been validated.

6.5.3 Documentation

Data migration thus relies on the third activity: **documentation**. No digital archivist can successfully preserve data that are not fully documented, because at every step of data migration information can be lost. This leaves archivists with two options: migrating data from one format and then double-checking each entry manually, or requiring thorough documentation of the data at the time of archiving so migrations can be carefully planned and tested in advance.

6.5.4 Data management tools

As already noted, digital data need to be regularly refreshed and migrated. Files that have been altered should move naturally into a localised back-up strategy, but where a deep storage facility is also employed (a preferred archival strategy where files are additionally stored in a remote and specialised repository) active intervention may be required for updating and version control. Thus digital archives need to be actively managed. Recommended data management tools include Electronic Document Management (EDM) systems that usually take the form of a database. Ideally the system employed will support the flagging of dates, which automatically inform the system manager when files need attention.

6.6 METADATA FOR RESOURCE DISCOVERY

6.6.1 Access and re-use

There is potentially a diverse audience for CAD models. Professionals, academics and researchers may want to find information about the results from previous projects. Another use for CAD models is by teaching professionals to support courses delivered in university departments and schools. Despite these potential uses, the *Survey of Archaeological Archives* (Swain 1998, 43–45) concluded that museum archives in general are a grossly under-utilised resource.

Use of archaeological archives is important for two reasons:
1   It facilitates communication within the discipline about work that has been undertaken
2   Sharing data helps in its preservation – the more formats a dataset is copied into, the greater the chance of it surviving.

One of the reasons given by the Swain report for the under-use of archives was difficulty in finding information about their location and contents. For example, the results of a survey of digital data (Condron *et al.* 1999, 29–32) suggest that CAD models may be retained by their creators or deposited with national agencies or local authorities, presenting difficulties for users who wish to identify their location. Increasingly users are turning to Internet gateways and search engines as a means of locating and accessing these data.

6.6.2 What is metadata?

Resource discovery metadata is the index-level information that is used by gateways through which users seek archival material. A resource discovery tool such as ArchSearch, the ADS online catalogue, makes information about digital archives available to potential users at the earliest possible opportunity. Different levels of digital data may be made available through such tools (Richards and Robinson 2000) and thus the available detail may be increased over time, as appropriate to the archaeological or academic significance of the project. Project managers are recommended to make simple metadata about each CAD model and its digital archive available as soon as possible following project completion. More detailed descriptive metadata or links to downloadable datasets may be added to this basic information at a later date.

6.6.3 The Dublin Core

The Archaeology Data Service, along with a growing number of organisations around the world, advocates use of the *Dublin Core* for recording the basic information that helps potential users to find and evaluate your data. This has been developed by an international consortium of academic and professional groups and provides a standard for the most basic metadata required.

The Dublin Core has evolved to become a series of fifteen broad categories, or elements. Each of these elements is *optional*, may be *repeated* as many times as required, and may be *refined* through the use of a developing set of sub-elements. The use of the Dublin Core within the Archaeology Data Service is discussed further elsewhere (Miller and Greenstein 1997; Wise and Miller 1997), and the current element definitions laid down across the Dublin Core community are available on the web.

6.6.4 Preparing metadata

As discussed above, it is important to contact the proposed digital archive at the outset of a project and to discuss requirements for making a deposit. Some digital archives may prepare the metadata, with the assistance of the project personnel. Others, such as the Archaeology

Information type	Scope note
Title	The name of the CAD model; this would normally refer to the name of the site.
Creator	Contact name and address for the person or organisation who created the model.
Subject	Keywords indexing the subject content of the dataset. They may be drawn from a standard terminology list, e.g. English Heritage's Thesaurus of Monument Types. If a local standard is used this should be included with the data set.
Description	A brief description of the main aims and objectives of the project from which the CAD model arose with a description of what the model itself shows.
Publisher	The organisation(s) who are providing access to the model. This may include: the digital archive or another organisation housing the model. With more commercial models, access may be made available according to stringent rules and regulations.
Date	The date(s) between which the model was produced.
Type	For example, CAD model.
Format	The format of the data file, e.g. DWG file.
Identifier	Unique identifying reference number for the resource.
Source	The source data for the model. CAD models may require multiple entries, one for each different set of source data: survey data, dimensional information from drawings, dimensional information from photogrammetry, surface colour or texture information from photographs, etc.

Table 2: CAD metadata for resource discovery (continued opposite)

Related archives	References to any published or unpublished sources, whether printed or machine-readable, or any other sources from which the data collection was derived (whether wholly or partially). Include details of where the sources are held and how they are identified (e.g. by accession number). If the data collection is derived from other sources, an indication should be included of whether it represents a complete or partial transcription/copy and the methodology used for its computerisation. Full references to any publications about or based upon the data collection should be included.
Language	For example, English.
Relation	This is important where the model is derived from a larger dataset or is related to other models (for example, which render a different aspect of the object).
Country	The country in which the site is located.
Spatial Coverage	National grid reference(s) for site
Administrative area	The county/unitary authority/district/parish in which the site is located.
Contributor	The name and address of the person(s) or organisation who deposited the data file.
Rights	The copyright to the model, normally held by the depositor, and user's rights of access.

Data Service, expect the data provider to provide the basic metadata. There may also be variations in the level of metadata requested; the Dublin Core metadata described above represent only the minimum requirement, and extra items may be added.

6.7 METADATA CASE STUDY

The metadata that is used in Internet gateways and search engines will be derived from the project documentation (see Section 5.2) and file level documentation (see Section 5.6) that is prepared for deposit with a digital archive. This documentation may be made available at different levels through the various gateways and search engines. For example, the metadata that is made available through ArchSearch (the ADS online catalogue) is based on the Dublin Core (see sub-section 6.6.3). Other gateways may make a reduced set of metadata available, or add additional descriptive elements.

Information type	Scope note
Title	Symon's Castle
Creator	Dr J. Huggett, Department of Archaeology, University of Glasgow, Dr C. Arnold
Subject	Motte and bailey castle
Subject	Palisade
Subject	Medieval
Description	Excavation of a 13th century AD timber and earthwork castle near Churchstoke, Powys. The project was directed by Dr C. Arnold and Dr J. Huggett over a 10-year period, on site for four weeks per year. The excavation was run as a training school for university students and other interested parties, and as a volunteer excavation. Although the site was largely undisturbed, the soil was very shallow and highly leached, requiring a modified recording procedure and full three-dimensional recording of artefacts.
Publisher	Dr J. Huggett, Department of Archaeology, University of Glasgow and Dr C. Arnold
Date	1985-1994
Type	Research level archive
Format	Documents - rtf
Format	AUTOCAD - dxf
Format	Images - jpg
Format	Images - gif
Identifier	Depositors ID: 1
Source	Symon's Castle project context plans, stone plans and topographic survey.
Related Archives	Plans: Department of Archaeology, University of Glasgow
Language	English
Relation	N/A
Country	Wales
Spatial coverage	SO 285 933
Administrative area	Churchstoke, Powys
Contributor	Dr J. Huggett, Department of Archaeology, University of Glasgow
Rights	Dr J. Huggett and Dr C. Arnold

Table 3: An example of a metadata record for Symon's Castle as it would appear in ArchSearch

Section 7: Depositing data from a CAD project in a digital archive

7.1 POSSIBLE DIGITAL ARCHIVE FACILITIES

A true archive is a repository with specific responsibilities and practices aimed at preserving items in perpetuity. One should not confuse a data processing centre with an archive. 'Corporate data processing centers, university computing centers, and other mainframe-based organizations understand issues of backup and refreshment of data, but don't necessarily understand the implications of real migration, particularly for more complex digital documents, or digital information within software environments that are still evolving rapidly and thus creating subtle kinds of obsolescence.' (Lyman and Besser 1998)

There are archives that specialise in archaeological data. In the United Kingdon there is the Archaeology Data Service. In the United States there is the Archaeological Research Institute at Arizona State University in Tempe, Arizona. Both of these institutions specialise in specific kinds of digital data.

Libraries, museums and other organisations also offer archive facilities but research suggests that most existing repositories are aware of, but have not yet confronted, the challenges of preserving digital datasets. Indeed the *Survey of Archaeological Archives in England* (Swain 1998, 47) concluded that 'most museums do not have the correct technology to store, access and curate in the long term those archives for which computer files play an important part'.

It should be the responsibility of those managing archaeological resources in a region to liaise over how best to manage the digital resource for their area (whether locally or through an agency such as the ADS) and then articulate this to contractors. We recommend that fieldworkers should consult with the museum, National Monuments Record, SMR, or other archive repository that will receive the rest of the project archive about their digital archiving policies. Contact the ADS for information if there is doubt about what to do with CAD archives.

7.2 REQUIREMENTS FOR DEPOSITING DATA WITH ARCHIVES

Archival preservation of CAD models may be required by funding agencies or professional organisations. Some guidelines about archiving are already mandatory for certain sectors within the discipline of archaeology in the UK, for example:

- Museum curators working in UK museums that are accredited by the Museums and Galleries Commission should adhere to the MGC (MGC 1992) and Society of Museum

Archaeologists (SMA 1993; 1995) guidelines for archive access, deposition, recording, and storage.

- Archaeologists funded by Historic Scotland must adhere to *Publication and Archiving of Archaeological Projects* (Historic Scotland 1996a) and the *Guidelines for Archiving of Archaeological Projects* (RCAHMS 1996).
- Projects funded by English Heritage must conform to the Guidelines known as MAP2 (English Heritage 1991).
- Projects in Wales should be aware of the developing strategy for archaeology in Wales (Cadw and RCAHMW 1998).
- Archaeologists creating digital data with funds received from the Arts and Humanities Research Board, British Academy, Council for British Archaeology, Leverhulme Trust, Natural Environment Research Council, Society of Antiquaries of London, or the Wellcome Trust should deposit digital archives with the Archaeology Data Service (ADS 1998).

Special archiving requirements are often included in project designs or specifications that vary on a case-by-case basis (e.g. Northamptonshire Heritage 1998).

7.3 GENERAL CONSIDERATIONS WHEN DEPOSITING DATA

Some digital archives have documented guidelines for depositors (see Section 7.4) but others set terms and conditions for each project and each new deposit. The best approach is always to contact the repository early in the project. It is possible that an archive might decline the data offered, where they are considered to be of limited relevance to the users of a particular repository or uniquely difficult to migrate. Different archives are also pursuing different approaches to underwriting the costs of archival storage and costs should be discussed at the outset.

7.3.1 The selection, retention and discard of CAD models

Many large projects make extensive use of CAD and during their life span literally thousands of CAD models may be created and saved as part of a project's archive. For example, CAD is often used to digitise the hand-drawn plans and sections from large archaeological excavation projects. An excavation may have thousands, or even tens of thousands, of individual contexts, each of which are often digitised and saved as a separate CAD file. During the process of post-excavation these files are often agglomerated into sets of group, sub-group and phase plans, and CAD models may be saved at each stage in the process. All of these later models are essentially composites of the earlier context plans. The appropriate use of a layer-naming system (see Section 4.3) can help to reduce the need for large numbers of separate files. Rather than generating new files each time, new layers can easily be added to existing models to reflect changes in interpretation and, in the process, maintain a close relationship between the underlying data and the interpretations derived from them.

At some point, all project managers need to consider the question of whether it is really necessary to archive and, of course, to document every model. There are obvious cost implications associated with these decisions. During the final stages of a project there should be a process of data selection, where the overall archive is worked through and individual files are either selected for retention in the archive or are discarded. This process is a standard part of the preparation of the non-digital project archive for deposition, and should also be part of how large digital archives are dealt with. For example, there are arguments to be made for the inclusion of every set of group, sub-group and phase plans in the archive, despite the fact that they are often simply agglomerations of the individual context plans. Essentially this will lead to a lot of duplication of data in the archive. Nevertheless such composite plans represent the cumulative results of interpretative decisions made by the archaeologists and as such are important building blocks towards the overall understanding of the site. Consequently it is important that these files are archived as they have a high re-use potential. It is also important that the individual context plans are archived alongside the group, sub-group and phase plans as they can be used to question the original archaeologists' phasing of the site and as such can be re-used to attempt radical re-interpretations of the archaeology.

Nevertheless, there will be CAD files that are appropriate to discard and omit from the final archival deposit. Such models include test and unfinished versions of later plans or earlier versions of phasing, which have been superseded by later interpretations and would consequently lead to false impressions of the archaeology of the site.

It is important to document the selection, retention and discard policy for a given project.

7.3.2 Data currency

The issues of which files to include in a final digital archive and which to leave out neatly brings us to the issues surrounding data currency. Often during the process of interpretation things change and there is not always time to go back to previous versions of files to bring them up to date. For example, during post-excavation interpretations evolve and those writing the site up tend to work from the latest version of the plans, so that previous versions become orphaned. Under such a scenario the individual context plans, once incorporated into sub-group or phase plans, may not be revisited. Consequently as interpretations change, older versions of files tend to become fossilised with the interpretations at the time of their last save. In an extreme case a sub-group may be initially thought to belong to a particular phase during post-excavation but additional information, such as refined dating evidence, may in fact mean that it belongs to a completely different phase. Such things happen; in the ideal world of course there would be a constant process of revision of earlier files to ensure that the entire archive is of the same currency. In the majority of cases, however, this would not be practical or financially viable. Consequently during the process of data selection, mentioned above, there should also be an assessment process during which the currency of the information contained in each file is considered. After this a policy of data revision may be put in place if time and cost constraints permit.

The presence of large volumes of orphaned CAD files within an archive could give a false picture of the archaeology of the site for the unwary user of the data. For some projects a programme of data revision may be out of the question, and consequently serious questions should be asked and the issue of whether such demonstrably flawed datasets should be retained or discarded from the digital archive must be confronted. Where the datasets still contain valuable information about the site, or where the archive would be seriously deficient without the inclusion of such files, it may be possible to retain orphaned CAD models as long as they are deposited with a 'health warning'. Such a warning should document which files are orphaned, why the information contained within them is not of the same currency of the rest of the archive and how they may be brought up to this level. The process of the creation of this documentation may be long and complicated and it may well be as time consuming as a programme of data revision. Nevertheless it is up to individual projects to reach a decision as to which policy is best for them.

7.3.3 Copyright

The data deposited with a repository may be the sole copyright of the depositor or copyright may be jointly held. Arrangements for fair use of the digital data will generally be specified at the time of deposit.

There are real difficulties in enforcing copyright of digital data. It is virtually impossible to detect some kinds of copyright violation and the legal framework for dealing with digital materials has not matured. Nonetheless copyright exists and should be asserted. In the case of commercially valuable data, legal advice should be sought at the time of deposit.

Some data sources used in preparing CAD models (e.g. maps, drawings and photographs) are likely to be copyrighted by others. Project directors must not only have permission to use these sources but they must be certain that all necessary permissions to use the new version of the data have been granted.

7.3.4 Data compression

Various data compression techniques are available and these can be divided into two categories: lossless and lossy data compression. The latter offers greater reduction in file size but also results in data loss. The data stored in an archive should not be compressed although lossless data compression techniques may sometimes be used to transfer data. If CAD files need to be compressed for data transfer, lossless compression software based on the Lempel-Ziv algorithm should be used. Applications include: Unix compress and uncompress, gzip and gunzip and WinZip.

Lossy compression techniques should only be used to disseminate files on the Internet, e.g. jpg images might be produced from screen shots of CAD models. DWF is generally used to publish CAD models on the Internet. To prevent the difficulties that could arise with improper data compression and extraction, project directors should plan to submit the uncompressed original files only and consult the digital archive before using any compression techniques.

7.4 DEPOSITING CAD DATA WITH THE ARCHAEOLOGY DATA SERVICE

The ADS archives, disseminates and catalogues high quality digital resources of long-term interest to archaeologists. Its geographical remit is to provide digital archiving facilities for archaeologists based in the UK. As many archaeologists based in academic institutions in the UK are engaged in research overseas, the scope of the ADS collections is international.

The ADS acknowledges that it is of considerable benefit to both depositors and users that there be an effective and rigorous process of peer review of materials proposed for accessioning.

In order to assist the ADS evaluate datasets and maintain the rigorous standards necessary for the effective development of a quality resource base, a Collections Evaluation Working Party has been set up.

Data resources that are offered for deposit to the ADS will be evaluated to:

- assess their intellectual content and the level of potential interest in their re-use
- evaluate how (even whether) they may viably be managed, preserved, and distributed to potential secondary users
- determine the presence or absence of another suitable archival home.

Whereas the first form of evaluation involves assessment of the content of a data resource, the second focuses more on data structure and format, and on the nature and completeness of any documentation supplied. The third evaluation criterion is intended to prevent duplication of digital archiving efforts within the archaeological community, and to preserve the integrity of existing digital archives. Such evaluation is essential to determine how best to manage a digital resource for the purpose of preservation and secondary re-use, and also to determine what costs may be involved in accessioning and migrating the digital resource. For further information please refer to the ADS Collections Policy.

7.4.1 Deposit formats

In the last few years many data formats have appeared that are intended to make data exchange and migration easier. Some of these formats are proprietary (i.e. they are marketed by a single company) but many are open standards that are independent of the software that is used. In general, open data formats are preferred for digital preservation. Although software manufacturers use open file formats they may occasionally change or extend them to cover new data types. Unfortunately this has the effect of making them less than 100% compatible with other software manufacturers who can take a while to catch up. It is best to check with a digital archive in the planning stages of any project to check if there are any concerns with the anticipated file formats.

The format in which you deposit data in depends on the type of information contained within. The Archaeology Data Service recommends the file formats outlined in Table 4 for delivery to the ADS, long-term preservation and for Internet dissemination. **Delivery formats** pertain to the file types that will be accepted by the ADS as a component of a deposit. Where necessary these delivery file formats will be migrated into a **Preservation** format for long-term storage and may also be converted to a **Dissemination** format for delivery over the Internet. Dissemination formats may also include widely used proprietary formats such as Microsoft Word and Adobe Acrobat files for texts and jpeg for images, which may have no long-term preservation potential. For CAD data, the ADS is able to accept AutoCAD files in DXF and DWG file formats. DXF, DWG and other native file formats can be accepted provided that they can be translated into AutoCAD DXF and DWG formats for long-term preservation. Files may also be translated to DWF for dissemination on the Internet.

Data type	Delivery formats	Preservation formats	Dissemination formats
CAD	DXF, DWG plus native file format	DXF, DWG	DXF, DWG, DWF
Databases	ASCII delimited text, MS Access (up to v. 2000), Paradox (up to v. 8), DBF	ASCII delimited text	ASCII delimited text
Geophysics	Contours, Geoplot, plain text (data + control info)	AGF, plain text (data + control info)	AGF, plain text (data + control info)
GIS	ArcInfo export, ArcInfo ungen, ArcInfo shapefile, DXF + DWG, ArcView (up to v. 3), MIF/MID, NTFF, SDTF, MOSS, VDF	ArcInfo, DXF, DWG	ArcInfo, DXF, DWG
Images	Uncompressed TIFF, BMP, JPEG, BIL, CGM, PNG, PhotoCD	Uncompressed TIFF (archival master)	BMP, JPEG
Spreadsheets	ASCII delimited text, Excel, Lotus123, Quattro Pro	ASCII delimited text	ASCII delimited text
Texts	ASCII text, RTF, HTML, PDF, Postscript, LaTeX, ODA, SGML, TeX, Word, WordPerfect	ASCII text, HTML	ASCII text, HTML, PDF, Word

Table 4: Delivery, preservation and dissemination file formats

7.4.2 Contacting the Archaeology Data Service

Please feel free to contact the ADS directly if you have any questions or concerns.

Archaeology Data Service
University of York
King's Manor
York YO1 7EP
Email: info@ads.ahds.ac.uk
Web: http://ads.ahds.ac.uk/

Bibliography and web references

BIBLIOGRAPHY

Archaeology Data Service, 1998, *Guidelines for Depositors*. Online: http://ads.ahds.ac.uk/project/ userinfo/deposit.html

—— 1999, *Collections Policy*. Online: http://ads.ahds.ac.uk/project/collpol3.html

—— 2000, *Charging Policy*. Online: http://ads.ahds.ac.uk/project/userinfo/charging2.html

Austin, T., Robinson, D. and Westcott, K. 2001, 'A Digital Future for our excavated past' in Z. Stancic and T. Veljanovski, 2001 *Computing Applications and Quantative Methods in Archaeology, Proceedings of the 28th Conference, Ljublijana, April 2000*, BAR International Series 931, 289–96.

Beagrie, N. and Greenstein, D. 1998, *A Strategic Policy Framework for Creating and Preserving Digital Collections*. Online: http://ahds.ac.uk/manage/framework.htm

Biswel, *et al.* 1995, 'GIS an excavation: a cautionary tale from Shepton Mallett, Somerset, England', in G. Lock and Z. Stancic (eds), *Archaeology and Geographical Information Systems*, Taylor and Francis, pp. 269–85.

Cadw and RCAHMW, 1998, *Strategy for Recording and Preserving the Archaeology of Wales*.

Condron, F., Richards, J., Robinson, D. and Wise, A. 1999, *Strategies for Digital Data – Findings and Recommendations from Digital Data in Archaeology: a Survey of User Needs*. Archaeology Data Service, York.

EEC, 1993, Directive 93/98/EEC of 29 October 1993 harmonizing the term of protection of copyright and certain related rights, *Official Journal of the European Union* L290.

Eiteljorg, H. II, 1988, *Computer-Assisted Drafting and Design: New Technologies for Old Problems*, CSA, Bryn Mawr.

—— 1990, 'Using the MR2 Program and Tolerating Frustration', *CSA Newsletter*, Vol. III, August 1990, no. 2, 3–5, CSA, Bryn Mawr.

—— 1993, *The Entrance to the Athenian Acropolis before Mnesicles*, Archaeological Institute of America Monograph, New Series, No. 1, Boston.

—— 1994, 'Using a Total Station', *CSA Newsletter*, Vol. VII, August 1994, no. 2, 7–10, CSA, Bryn Mawr.

—— 1995, 'New total station – Surveying in Pompeii', *CSA Newsletter*, Vol. VIII, August 1995, no. 2, 5–10, CSA, Bryn Mawr.

—— 1996a, 'New survey aids', *CSA Newsletter*, Vol. IX, May 1996, no. 1, 10, CSA, Bryn Mawr.

—— 1996b, 'Pompeii in 1996', *CSA Newsletter*, Vol. IX, August 1996, no. 2, 5–7, CSA, Bryn Mawr.

—— 1996c, 'Accurate, efficient surveying with MR2 Program', *CSA Newsletter*, Vol. IX, August 1996, no. 2, 1–3, CSA, Bryn Mawr.

—— 2000, 'The compelling computer image – a double-edged sword' *Internet Archaeology* Issue 8 http://intarch.ac.uk/journal/issue8/eiteljorg_toc.html

—— 2002a, 'Linking text and data to CAD models', *CSA Newsletter*, Vol. XIV, Winter 2002, no 3, CSA, Bryn Mawr.

—— 2002b, *The CSA CAD Guide for Archaeologists and Architectural Historians*, June 2002, CSA, Bryn Mawr. Online: http://csanet.org/inftech/cadgd/cadgd.html

English Heritage, undated, *The Presentation of Historic Building Survey in CAD*, English Heritage

—— 1991, *Management of Archaeological Projects*, 2nd edition.

—— 2000, *Metric Survey Specification for English Heritage*, English Heritage.

Gillings, M. and Wise, A. (eds) 1998, *GIS Guide to Good Practice*. Arts and Humanities Data Service, London. Online: http://ads.ahds.ac.uk/project/goodguides/gis/

Historic Scotland, 1996a, *Historic Scotland Operational Policy Paper #2: Publication and Archiving of Archaeological Projects*.

—— 1996b, *Project Design, Implementation and Archiving*.

HMSO, 1988, *The Copyright, Design and Patents Act*, London.

Huggett, J. 1989, 'Computing and the Deansway Archaeology Project', *Archaeological Computing Newsletter*, no. 18, 1–7, Oxford.

—— 1990, 'Programming AutoCAD for the archaeologist', *Archaeological Computing Newsletter*, no. 25, 18–24, Oxford.

Huggett, J. and Chen, G-Y. 2000, '3-D interpretative modelling of archaeological sites: A computer reconstruction of a medieval timber and earthwork castle' *Internet Archaeology* Issue 8, http://intarch.ac.uk/journal/issue8/huggett_index.html

Jones, S. C. 1997, 'Raster and vector images – an important distinction', *CSA Newsletter*, Vol. X, Spring 1997, no. 1, 7–8, CSA, Bryn Mawr.

Institute of Field Archaeologists, 1999a, *Standard and Guidance for Archaeological Excavation* Online: http://www.archaeologists.net/docs/codes/exc2.pdf

—— 1999b, *Appendix 2 Preparation of Specification* Online: http://www.archaeologists.net/docs/codes/standards_appendix.pdf

—— 1999c, *Appendix 3 Contents of Project Design* Online: http://www.archaeologists.net/docs/codes/standards_appendix.pdf

Lavender, D., Wallis, A., Bowyer, B. and Davenport, P. 1990, 'Solid modelling of Roman Bath', in P. Reilly and S. Rahtz (eds), *Communication in Archaeology: a global view of the impact of information technology*, Volume 1: Data Visualisation, pp. 7–13, IBM UK Scientific Centre, Winchester.

Lyman, P. and Besser, H. 1998, 'Defining the problem of our vanishing memory: Background, current status, models for resolution', in M. MacLean and B. H. Davis (eds), *Time and Bits: Managing Digital Continuity*, pp.11–20, J. Paul Getty Trust.

McGregor, C. C. 2000, 'A virtual reconstruction of the inner enclosure of the Temple of Tutu, Dakhleh Oasis, Egypt', *Archaeological Computing Newsletter*, no. 56, Autumn 2000, 7–16 Oxford.

Miller, P. and Greenstein, D. 1997, *Discovering Online Resources Across the Humanities: A Practical Implementation of the Dublin Core*. Bath: UKOLN.

Miller, P. and Richards, J. 1995, 'The good, the bad, and the downright misleading: archaeological adoption of computer visualisation', in J. Huggett and N. Ryan (eds), *Computer Applications and Quantitative Methods in Archaeology 1994*, BAR International Series 600, 19–22.

Museums and Galleries Commission, 1992, *Standards in the Museum Care of Archaeological Collections*.

Northamptonshire Heritage, 1998, *Data Standards and Guidance for Digital Data Transfer to the Northamptonshire SMR*, Northamptonshire Heritage

RCAHMS, 1996, *Guidelines for Archiving of Archaeological Projects*

RCHME, 1995 *Thesaurus of Monument Types: a data standard for use in archaeological and architectural records.*

Richards, J. D. and Robinson, D. J. (eds), 2000, *Digital Archives from Excavation and Fieldwork: A Guide to Good Practice*, 2nd edition, Archaeology Data Service. Online: http://ads.ahds.ac.uk/project/goodguides/excavation/

Society of Museum Archaeologists, 1993, *Selection, Retention and Dispersal of Archaeological Collections: Guidelines for use in England, Wales and Northern Ireland.*

—— 1995, *Towards an Accessible Archive. The Transfer of Archaeological Archives to Museums: Guidelines for Use in England, Northern Ireland, Scotland and Wales.*

Swain, H. 1998, *A Survey of Archaeological Archives in England, English Heritage and Museums and Galleries Commission*, London

Templeton, L. 1990, 'Archaeological illustration and Computer-Aided Design', *Archaeological Computing Newsletter* no. 24, 1–8, Oxford.

Wheatley, P. 2001, 'Migration – a CAMiLEON discussion paper', *Ariadne* Issue 29, www.ariadne.ac.uk/issue29/camileon/

Wise, A. L. and Miller, P. 1997, Why Metadata Matters in Archaeology, *Internet Archaeology* 2, http://intarch.ac.uk/journal/issue2/wise_index.html.

INFORMATION ABOUT CAD ON THE WEB

OpenDWG Alliance http://www.opendwg.org/index.htm The OpenDWG™ Alliance is an association of CAD customers and vendors committed to promoting Autodesk's AutoCAD DWG drawing file format as an open, industry-standard format for the exchange of CAD drawings.

Dublin Core http://dublincore.org/documents/1998/09/dces/ Dublin Core Metadata Element Set, Version 1.0: Reference Description.

Glossary

3-D – three-dimensional, that is reference to a position using all cartesian axes (x, y and z).

3-point perspective – a perspective drawing made with three vanishing points, one for each axis.

Base data – usually used to relate to unmodified photogrammetric data.

CAD – an acronym for computer-aided (assisted) drafting or computer-aided (assisted) design. CAD software is used to design or document physical structures or objects.

Close-range photogrammetry – photogrammetry practised with the aid of computing power, permitting non-stereo photographs from non-rectified cameras to be used to generate fully three-dimensional survey data. Sometimes called desktop photogrammetry. Digital photographs may be used with some programs.

Cross-section – a cut profile taken across the subject.

Database link – a connection between a CAD drawing entity and a record or row in a database.

Desktop photogrammetry – see close-range photogrammetry.

Digitise – the process of converting hard-copy line drawings or phtographs into a digital format using a digitiser.

Digital terrain model – a DTM is a digital representation of a three-dimensional surface that is modelled from XYZ coordinates. DTMs are normally used to model landscapes.

Digitiser – a data input device with a tablet and cursor. The tablet has a defined surface and it is possible to relate position on the tablet to position in a coordinate system or even to scale the tablet surface in order to trace drawings.

Digitising tablet – see digitiser

Drawing entity – a CAD model consists of a great many lines, circles, points, surfaces, and so on. Each may be called a drawing entity, providing a convenient term to refer to any piece of a large model without specifying its character.

DXF – drawing exchange format. A file format for the exchange of CAD information. Although the DXF format is public, changes are made to the specifications by Autodesk without consultation.

DWG – AutoCAD's native file format for CAD models.

EDM – an Electronic Distance Measure is a surveying device which transmits and receives an electromagnetic signal to measure distance by comparing the wavelengths of the two signals. Short-range EDMs transmit signals in the visible infrared part of the electromagnetic spectrum.

Elevation – a drawing of the vertical face of a building, wall, or other object. Such a drawing has no three-dimensionality and is simply a plan view of a vertical surface.

Engineering drawing – a drawing consisting of at least three views (front, top, and right side) of an object. Certain conventions are normally used to indicate hidden parts of the object; the point is to specify the object fully with simple plan views of the visible surfaces. Views of other surfaces may be necessary, as may cross-sectional views. Dimensions are normally provided.

File format – the way information is recorded in a computer data file. Specifications of a format permit the file to be written according to a standard and then retrieved for use or alteration.

Hand survey – the collection of information by hand measurement.

Hidden-line view – a three-dimensional model which hides from view lines which would in real-life be obscured by objects in front of them.

Instrument survey – the use of theodolite, EDM, total station etc. to record the location of points and lines in a common coordinate system.

Isometric drawing – a three-dimensional drawing made without the effects of vanishing points or foreshortening. In an isometric drawing parallel lines receding into space remain parallel (rather than appearing to converge as in a perspective drawing), and scale along any individual axis is consistent from foreground to background (rather than diminishing as in a perspective drawing).

Isometric view – a three-dimensional view of an object without foreshortening.

Layer – CAD files normally divide their contents into segments that may be displayed or drawn on command, making it possible to see only specific parts of a model at one time. These data segments are called layers. Layers need not have physical boundaries but may be entirely conceptual.

Migrate – to change data from one file format to another.

Line type – the generation of identifiable line patterns by CAD.

Measured survey – a non-photographic survey, applying draughting skills within a controlled framework.

Metric survey – the acquisition of data by the use of a controlled and repeatable method. It includes measured survey and photogrammetric survey.

Model – a CAD use, a complex representation of some particular physical reality in computer form. The term is used in place of *drawing*, because many drawings could be created from a CAD model. A three-dimensional model is obviously too complex to be considered a drawing, since changing the point of view changes the drawing. A complex object drawn with multiple layers is also too complex to be considered a single drawing even if it is a simple, two-dimensional representation; changing the visible layers changes the drawing but not the model.

Parametric solid – a geometric model which can be surfaced.

Photogrammetric survey – production of drawings and maps using stereo-photography and survey control.

Photo rectification – process of altering a photograph to change the apparent angle of view. An oblique-angled photograph is rectified when it is altered so that the apparent angle is head-on, and the correct geometric relationships between and among portions of the whole are preserved. (See plane transformation.)

Plot – a generic term used to describe the production of hard-copies from a CAD model.

Pin-bar drafting – drafting on multiple sheets of paper (some of which are transparent) with the the use of registration pins to align the paper. Each drawing sheet contains a different portion of the whole, and the pins allow all to be aligned identically. Thus, when combined, the drawings show the full complexity of the object, but they show individual aspects when viewed separately

Pixel – one individual, discrete point on a computer screen, the smallest element of the image made on a screen. (See raster.)

Plane transformation – the mathematical process of translating positions from one plane to another by knowing that certain points in each of the two planes can be matched to one another, making it possible to map all points on one plane to equivalent points on another. (See photo rectification.)

Plotter – a device for making a large paper drawing from a CAD program. Several varieties of plotters are now available. Older models use pens on an armature and moving paper. Newer ones use electrostatic charges or ink-jet technology to put ink on paper.

Raster (image) – images on cathode ray tube devices (televisions or computer monitors) are created by closely spaced scanning lines that consist themselves of closely-spaced dots. Raster refers to the scanning pattern and is used in general to indicate an image made of individual dots rather than lines, circles, arcs, letters, and so on. (See pixel; compare vector.)

Rectified photography – photography taken in such a way, or subsequently corrected, to provide a scaled image of the subject.

Refresh – to write a data file onto new media in order to counter the effects of magnetic decay.

Scale – the ratio between the subject and its representation when plotted.

Scan – to create an electronic image of a paper document or object with a device attached to a computer (a scanner). The electronic image is a raster image.

Scale of tolerance – the ratio between the subject and its representation when plotted.

Sectional elevation – the elevational view seen if a line of cut is taken across part of a building.

Solid model – a model that includes specific information about solid objects, not simply surfaces. Solid models permit realistic views, since surfaces may be included, but they also permit calculations of object weight, centre of gravity, and the like.

Surface model – a model that includes specified surfaces. It is possible to make a realistic view of such a model, since surfaces have been specified, and it is possible to determine which lines (or parts of lines) would be hidden by those surfaces.

Surface normal – the exposed side of a surface. Many programs for rendering are designed to render only the surface that is exposed or visible (any defined surface is actually two surfaces, one faced in one direction and the other faced in the opposite direction 180 degrees away) so as to save the time required to render the invisible surface. The surface normal is the face intended to be seen (and rendered). (Surfaces can be defined by a series of points defining the edge. Viewed from one side, the points will have been entered in a clockwise direction; from the other side they will have been entered in an anti- or counter-clockwise direction. The side showing those points to have been entered in anti- or counter-clockwide direction is considered the surface normal.)

Total station – a surveying device consisting of an electronic theodolite and a coupled electronic distance measuring device. The total station may also include a data recorder for retaining individual measurements (swing angle, angle on inclination, and distance to target). The total station itself will generally be able to calculate point positions, as will the data recorder, but the data recorder is required to store the information and to transfer that information to a computer.

Vector – a mathematical representation of the shape of a line, arc, or circle, indicating coordinate starting point, direction of travel and distance of travel. A vector image is a screen or paper image generated from the mathematical representations of the drawing entities. The scale of the image can be enlarged or reduced to any size desired, and the image will still be correctly shown.

Vectorise – to turn an image consisting only of pixels (a raster image) into an image generated from vectors.

Virtual reality (VR) – a general term used to indicate some form of extremely life-like computer representation. Some would restrict use of the term to computer-generated environments that are immersive; the 'visitor' wears goggles with projected images and is positioned in a room such that he can simulate movement in space. Movement will be reflected in the goggles, and he/she may even have gloves with sensors so that movement of the hands can be reflected in the goggles. Others would broaden the term to include very life-like computer displays that may be manipulated in real time.

Wire-frame – a three-dimensional outline CAD drawing, often the result of an instrument survey. This can be used as an armature or framework.

Appendix 1: Accuracy and instrument tests

There are two principal methods of testing the accuracy of measurements; calibration and repeatability.

Calibration involves testing instruments to make certain that no errors are introduced. For example an instrument may be adjusted so that a measurement or reading conforms to a known standard.

Repeatability involves taking measurements more than once to be sure that the results are consistent. A repeatable measurement should be a good one if the instruments have been checked and the personnel properly trained.

Measurement tests – Tape measures can be tested against a standard measure of known length. Total stations can be tested as follows:

- With a one-second machine with a one-millimetre EDM, any measurement should have less than 2mm error even if measuring from 100 metres away. This error will still be under 10mm at a kilometre distant.
- With a five-second machine and a three-millimetre EDM, any measurement should have about a 3mm error at a measuring distance of 10 metres and less than 5mm at a measuring distance of 100m.

Digitisers can be tested as follows:

Place a mark on a piece of paper taped to a digitiser surface and then select the mark ten times in a row – looking away between each choice. Comparing the actual coordinates of the points will show the limit on accuracy when tracing from drawings and suggest the level of acceptable precision if a drawing is to be used for data input.

Determining instrument tolerances – Using the tangent of the maximum angular measurement error and the distance from total station to measured point provides a number for maximum position error in one direction. Since the same error can occur in both horizontal and vertical directions, one must then imagine a square with the real point at one corner and the maximum error at the opposite corner; the diagonal of the square would then provide the maximum error introduced by angular measurement. To the angular measurement error must be added the distance measurement error (this time using the diagonal of an imaginary rectangle). In any case, the potential error due to angular mis-measurement is very small when compared to the error that may occur in the distance measurement (Eiteljorg 2002b).

Appendix 2: The CSA layer-naming convention

The CSA layer-naming convention is based on layer names designed to specify the contents of each layer clearly. These make it possible to search for layers or groups of layers using the standard 'wild card' database searches permitting quick and efficient access to layers without having to remember individual names.

Each letter in the layer name designates information according to its position as well as the letter itself. The scheme permits the use of letters of the alphabet and the numerals 1 to 9 (not

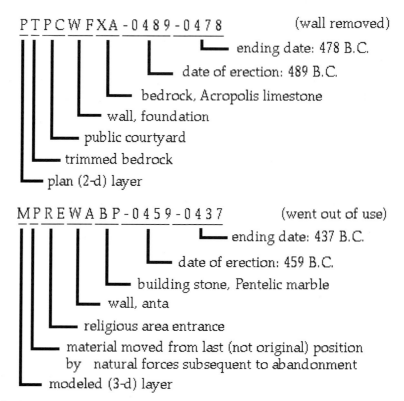

Figure 22: Two examples of layer names from a model of the Acropolis entrance

0) for each position in the name. The dash/minus sign and the numerals 0 to 9 inclusive may be used for the dates.

Coding the description

The eight characters used to describe what has been drawn on a layer are:

1 Indicates the kind of drawing layer, e.g. icons, 3-D model of artefacts, cracks, database links, dimensions, holes in a surface, labels, 3-D modelled surfaces, notes, 2-D plan, solid models, texture.

2 Indicates whether the feature/object was found *in situ*, had been disturbed, was a random find, was found *in situ* but moved from its last point of use, is hypothetical or is a natural feature etc.

3 Designates the general type of the area, e.g. public, domestic, military, work/manufacturing area, agricultural etc.

4 Designates the specific part of an area (dependent on character 3), e.g. hall, anteroom, meeting place, kiln, etc.

5 Indicates the general nature of the feature, e.g. buttress, column, pillar/post, gate, monument, pavement/floor, roof, stair, entablature, wall, etc.

6 Indicates specific nature of the feature (dependent on character 5), e.g. base, capital, mosaic, etc.

7 Indicates general material, e.g. animal fibre, building stone, concrete, bone, unbaked clay, metal, plant fibre, rough stone, worked stone, terracotta, mudbrick, wood, bedrock, etc.

8 Indicates the specific material (dependent on character 7), e.g. oak, obsidian, wool.

Coding the dates

For each layer there are two dates, one defining the earliest date attached to material placed on the layer and one defining the latest date. There are ten characters for dates, five for a starting date and five for an ending date and unused spaces are filled with leading zeroes. BC dates include a minus sign in the first position. AD dates have an extra leading zero. This system only permits dates as far back as 9999 BC using the minus sign, but it could be adapted for earlier dates.

Dates are 'rounded' to enable searching, thus a date in the first quarter of the 5th century BC is included in the layer name -0499 (start date) -0475 (end date).

Notes

Some material may exist on more than one layer; for example a triglyph found re-used in a secondary context could be modelled and positioned on one layer identified by its find spot and on another layer identified by the date and structure from which it is thought to have come.

The CSA layer-naming scheme described is an analytic scheme which may work less well for excavations in progress. Too much knowledge is presupposed by the system and different schemes may be used by excavators, e.g. separating material according to excavator, season, trench, etc.

A full explanation of the CSA layer-naming system is available on line at the Center for the Study of Architecture website. The document provides both a general explanation of the way naming layers can enhance any project and a more specific set of suggestions.

Appendix 3: The English Heritage layer-naming convention

English Heritage has developed the following layer-naming convention published in *The Presentation of Historic Building Survey in CAD* for a number of survey types (English Heritage, undated and English Heritage, 2000).

English Heritage uses a coding system for layer naming. Each name is constructed of two fields, the first describes the author of the layer by discipline, the second contains an abbreviated description of the entities held in that layer.

- Field 1: Discipline code
- Field 2: Category code

Authors of layers are divided into source disciplines (the producers of primary measured survey) and user disciplines (the end users). The discipline codes are:

Source Discipline	Code	User Discipline	Code
Photogrammetry	OP-	Architectural design	AD-
Architectural survey	OA-	Architectural history	AH-
Topographic survey	OT-	AM Laboratory	AML-
Other sources	OM-	Building Archaeology	BA-
Digitised plans	OS-	Engineering	ENG-
Digital sources	OD-	Facilities management	FM-
Excavation archaeology	OX-	Landscape architects	L-
		Landscape historians	LH-
		Quantity surveyors	QS-

Lists of category codes as used in English Heritage are as follows:

Category codes for photogrammetric survey

Layer	Colour	Description
OP-1	White	MAJOR - include all structural elements, facing stone, ashlar, etc. except those specified for layers OP-2 to OP-6.
OP-2	Red	COREWORK - where exposed by facing stone no longer existing.

OP-3	Yellow	WINDOWS/DOORS/FIREPLACES - to include all jambs, sills, voussoirs, lintels and the surrounding stonework
OP-4	Green	ARCHITECTURAL FRAGMENTS - corbels, architrave, mouldings.
OP-5	Cyan	SCULPTURAL DETAIL - figures and carved detail
OP-6	Magenta	MODERN SERVICES - drainpipes, lightening conductors, ducting etc.
OP-7	Blue	TEXT/NOTES - relating to architectural data, not border information.
OP-8	White	CONTROL POINTS - a cross with point number, layer to be frozen.
OP-9 to OP-20		To remain blank unless used for an architectural element that doesn't fit into the above layers, the layer name to be prefixed by op- followed by name of detail

NOTES:

- Where architectural fragments or sculptural features form part of a window or door, etc. they are to appear within layer OP-3.
- When cross-sectional information is to be provided, the layering convention to be applied is to be applied to these sections, depending upon the type of detail that the cross-section passes through.
- Any areas of erosion or damage should be placed with the associated feature
- If there is any doubt about a feature it should be put into layer OP-1

Category codes for architectural survey

Layer	Colour	Description
OA-CNTL STATION	Yellow	Occupied stations
OA-CNTL POINT	Red	Detail point or node
OA-TRAVERSE	Yellow	Traverse lines, station locations and coordinates
OA-CONSTRUCTION		Construction lines. Centres etc.
OA-ANNOTATION		Text to be included in presentation
OA-TITLES		Text for sheet/drawing title
OA-GRID	Yellow	Datum lines and height indexing etc.
OA-ELEV-(N,S,E,W) FACE		Walls shown in elevation
OA-CUT LINE/MASTER LINE	Cyan	Walls in plan where cut by plan height
OA-OUT LINE	Magenta	Outline outside wall line, edge of plane etc.

OA-GROUND LINE	Cyan	Ground line
OA-DETAIL-20 OA-DETAIL-50		1:20 scale, all lines below or beyond the cut. For 1:50 scale as above.
OA-ROOF		All roof timbers
OA-OVERHEAD		Dashed lines for overhead detail
OA-RECONSTRUCT		Reconstructed lines
OA-SUPPLEMENTARY		Supplementary layer
OA-SOURCE-DIGI		Digitised data from other drawings
OA-SOURCE-OS		Ordnance Survey digital data
OA-SOURCE-PHOTO		Digitised data from photographs

Layer names for use in the survey of roofs

Layer	Colour	Description
OA-RIDGE	Yellow	The ridge board
OA-RAFTER	Yellow	Rafters
OA-PRAFTER	Red	Principal rafter
OA-TRUSS	Red	Truss and tie beam
OA-PURLIN	Green	Purlins to be expanded to PURLINU and PURLINL for upper and lower purlins
OA-HIP	Yellow	Hip board
OA-LAYBD		Layboard
OA-VALBD		Valley board
OA-WP		Wall plate
OA-CH	Cyan	Chimney
OA-DRAG	Red	Dragon tie

Layer names for use in the survey of vaults

Layer	Colour	Description
OA-CL		Centre line
OA-SL		Springing line
OA-VAULT		Completed vaulted cell (in 2-D) VAULTN, VAULTS, etc. to be used in 3-D work to separate elevational views line type: Dashed on plans (2-D) 3-D polyline for sectional views and 3-D work.
OA-RIB		Rib of vault

OA-RIBD		Diagonal rib
OA-CORB		Corbel; it will be necessary to have each face of the corbel in a separate layer so that logical views can be prepared from 3-D data
OA-SHAFT		Supporting shaft
OA-CAP		Capital, impost or abacus

Category codes for building archaeology

Layer	Colour	Line-type	Description
BA-BORD	Cyan	con	title/border
BA-IS	Blue	con	ironstone
BA-SS	Yellow	con	sandstone
BA-LS	Red	con	limestone
BA-FL	Red/20	con	flint
BA-CH	White	con	chert (silcrete)
BA-MA	Magenta	con	marble
BA-SL	Blue	con	slate
BA-TB	Blue	con	timber
BA-TI	Red/242	con	tile
BA-BR1	Magenta	con	brick
BA-BR2	Magenta	con	brick
BA-CON	White	con	concrete
BA-COR	Red	con	core
BA-MO1	Red/154	hatch/con	mortar
BA-MO2	Red/154	hatch/con	mortar
BA-GAL	White	con	galleting
BA-PL1	Green/91	hatch/con	plaster
BA-PL2	Green/91	hatch/con	plaster
BA-REN	Red/154	hatch/con	render
BA-LI1	Blue	hatch/con	limewash
BA-LI2	blue	hatch/con	limewash
BA-PA1	Red/84	solid/con	paint
BA-PA2	Red/84	solid/con	paint
BA-PA4	Blue	con	setting out lines
BA-MAS1	White	hatch/con	tooling
BA-MAS2	White	hatch/con	tooling
BA-GRAF	White	con	graffiti

BA-HUN	White	hatch/con	hungry joint
BA-REC	Blue	con	cut recess
BA-STRU	Cyan	con	structural feature
BA-TXR	Blue	con	text, recess depth
BA-TXO	Blue	con	text, offsets
BA-TXA	Blue	con	text, architectural stone
BA-TXD	Blue	con	text, other dimensions
BA-TXN	White	con	text, notes
BA-TXS	Blue	con	text, samples
BA-TCON	Blue	con	text, contexts
BA-TXT	White	con	text, title
BA-DE1	Magenta	hatch/con	decay under 10mm
BA-DE2	Magenta	hatch/con	decay over 10mm
BA-DE3	Blue	hatch/con	contour spalling
BA-DE4	Red	hatch/con	flaking
BA-DE5	Red	hatch/con	other decay
BA-DAM	White/211	con	damage
BA-LD1	White	con	Outline/limit of survey
BA-LD2	White	dashed 2	ground level
BA-LD3	White	dashed	obscured detail
BA-LD4	Cyan	dashdot	line of section
BA-Fe	Red	hatch/con	iron
BA-Pb	Grey/8	hatch/con	lead
BA-Cu	Yellow	hatch/con	copper
BA-CP	Cyan	con	change of plane
BA-PT	White	pdmode 34	survey point/control
BA-VEG	Green	con	vegetation
BA-WIN	Yellow	con	windows/doors
BA-SER	Green	con	services
BA-DWG	White	con	drawing conventions
BA-PUR	White	con	purbeck marble
BA-C	Grey/9	con	chalk
BA-GRAN	Magenta	con	granite
BA-PO	White	con	portland stone
BA-RAG	Green	con	ragstone
BA-GRAG	Green	con	green ragstone
BA-OYS	White	con	oyster shell

BA-CAEN	Yellow	con	caen stone
BA-SSI	Yellow	con	white sandstone
BA-ST	Grey/9	con	schist
BA-AS	Magenta	con	asphalt
BA-TU	Blue	con	tuffa
BA-YS	White	con	yorkstone
BA-#	White	con	context
BA-#	White	con	context

Category codes for topographic survey

Layer	Colour	Description
OT-35	Cyan	Lines to be plotted in a 0.35mm width; the line of cut plans. The pen should be offset on the inside of the building line so that the edge of the line describing the wall surface indicates the true wall position.
OT-025	Red	Lines to be plotted in a 0.25 or Yellow 0.18mm width; lines indicating information remote from the line of cut.
OT-CUT	Cyan	The line of section as it strikes all features, describing the vertical plane.
OT-DASHED	White	Lines to be plotted in a broken line type in a 0.25mm pen indicating overhead detail on plan, hidden detail below the line of cut or obscured in sectional elevation.
OT-DOT	White	To be used to describe 'indicative' information eg the position of lost building components. Pen: 0.25mm. Line type: Dot.
OT-TXT	Yellow	All text except title, logo title panel control text, tree data and text associated with height. Text associated with grid should be on layer GRIDTXT. Pen width of 0.25m.
OT-DIGII		To be used to separate digitised data from primary survey, to be expanded to DIGI2, DIGI3 etc. to accommodate line type. Colour should agree with line type and pen thickness.
OT-HT	Yellow	Spot levels to three decimal places if possible with associated text rotated so that it is visible wih all layers on. Pen: 0.25 or 0.18mm.
OT-Tree	Green	Tree bole hatched solid.
OT-FMAT25	White	Pen: 0.25mm, Main title 0.35m (Cyan).
OT-LEVEL	White	Level point descriptor.
OT-LVLTXT	White	Text for levels

OT-CONTOUR	Green	Contours to be plotted in 0.18mm or 0.13mm pen.
OT-CONTOUR-INDEX	Red	Index contours to be in 0.25mm pen. To be broken to accept text.
OT-HTG	Magenta	Ground line, a line at the base of a batter or where height of ground becomes part of the building plan.
OT-CORHL		Lines used to describe wall tops inside the line of cut, i.e. the view of the wall looking down from above.
OT-SERVICES-ELEC	Red	Electrical services, to be expanded as required.
OT-SERVICES-FIRE	Red	Fire control services.
OT-SERVICES-GAS	Blue	Gas services.
OT-SERVICES-WATER	121	Water supply.
OT-SERVICES-DRAIN-FOUL	34	Drainage, foul; show direction of flow
OT-SERVICES-DRAIN-RW	175	Drainage, rainwater; show direction of flow.
OT-SERVICES-TELE	Yellow	Telephone lines, poles to be shown, lines to be shown as an overhead detail with a dashed line.

Appendix 4: Standards in Archaeology

CONTENT STANDARDS

FISH – The Forum on Information Standards in Heritage. FISH exists to promote and develop standards covering the compilation and organisation of archaeological and architectural heritage 'inventories' (online: http://www.mda.org.uk/FISH/). The work of FISH has two complimentary starting points, MIDAS and INSCRIPTION:

- **MIDAS: A Manual and Data Standard for Monument Inventories**. Developed by RCHME in 1998 to assist in the creation of monument inventories such as Sites and Monuments Records (SMRs), and is an indispensable resource for archaeologists working in England. (Online: http://www.rchme.gov.uk/midas/index.html).

- **INSCRIPTION** provides a foundation for developing terminology control in monument inventories and related digital resources (online: http://www.mda.org.uk/fish/inscript.htm). It is particularly relevant in the light of the MIDAS standard which provides a standardised recording framework in which these terms may be deployed. It is not a wordlist or thesaurus in its own right so much as a definitive set of controlled vocabularies for a variety of purposes. It is recommended that INSCRIPTION approved terms are utilised in the documentation of CAD surveys, for example Monument Types should be drawn from either the English Thesaurus of Monument Types or the forthcoming Scottish Thesaurus of Monument Types, where appropriate.

The wordlists are organised by MIDAS units of information and include:

- ALGAO Event types (surveys)
- Event types (interpretation)
- Defence of Britain Thesaurus
- Thesaurus of Monument Types
- RCHME Thesaurus of building materials
- RCHME Archaeological Periods list
- Date range qualifier
- Evidence thesaurus
- Archaeological archive types

- REP93 Condition

- Currency

- Internal cross reference qualifiers

- REP93 Land use

- REP93 Topology

- English civil parishes

- English County list

- English district areas

- English non-parish areas

- English unitary authorities

In addition to the standards included in the INSCRIPTION word lists, there are a number of other important content standards that have relevance to the CAD practitioner.

- **Guide to the Description of Architectural Drawings**. This guide provides a general introduction to the principles of documenting architectural materials with recommendations for both digital and manual systems. Developed by the Getty Information Institute and partners (Online: http://www.getty.edu/research/institute/standards/fda/index.html).

PROFESSIONAL STANDARDS

Institute of Field Archaeologists (IFA) The IFA is the professional organisation for UK archaeologists (Online: http//www. archaeologists.net). It promotes professional standards and ethics for conserving, managing, understanding and promoting enjoyment of the heritage. The IFA has constitutional Codes of Conduct and Bylaws for:

- Area and special interest groups

- By-laws amplifying Articles 9–11 and defining 'competence'

- Code of approved practice for the regulation of contractual arrangements in field archaeology

- Code of conduct

- Disciplinary regulations

- Regulations for the Registration of archaeological organisations

The IFA is concerned with setting standards in archaeology. To date it has standards documents pertaining to:

- Desk-based assessment

- Field evaluation

- Watching brief

- Excavation

- Buildings investigation and recording

- Finds

The standards documents have several useful appendices that document items to cover in:

- Project specification

- Project design

- Post-excavation project design

Management of Archaeological Projects (MAP2). This standard document was developed by English Heritage as a guide to the management of all phases of archaeological projects. MAP2 includes guidelines for planning, fieldwork, assessment of potential, analysis, report preparation, and archiving (Online: http://www.eng-h.gov.uk/guidance/map2/).

ARCHIVAL AND OTHER USEFUL STANDARDS

Digital Archives from Excavation and Fieldwork: *A Guide to Good Practice*. The primary aim of this Digital Archiving Guide to Good Practice is to provide information on the best way to create and document digital material produced in the course of excavation and fieldwork, and to deposit it safely in a digital archive facility for future use. It was written by the ADS with contributions from a wide range of authors. (Online: http://ads.ahds.ac.uk/project/goodguides/ excavation).

   Elib Standards Guidelines (Version 2) This covers, concisely, a wide range of electronic format and interchange standards, and includes references to more detailed reading (Online http://www.ukoln.ac.uk/services/elib/papers/other/standards)

   Core Data Index to Historic Buildings and Monuments of the Architectural Heritage. Developed by the Council of Europe for architectural recording (Online: http://www.coe.fr/ index.htm).

   International Core Data Standard for Archaeological Sites and Monuments (Draft). Produced by CIDOC, the International Documentation Committee of the International Council of Museums, this document guides the user in documenting archaeological sites and monuments. The goal of this standard is to facilitate international exchange of information by encouraging standardised approaches to database structure (Online: http//www.natmus.min.dk/cidoc/archsite/ coredata/arch1.htm).

   JISC/TLTP Copyright Guidelines. This document is targeted at the HE audience and covers a wide range of copyright issues in electronic media . (Online: http://www.ukoln.ac.uk/ services/elib/papers/other/jisc-tltp/jisc.pdf).

Recording Historic Buildings: A Descriptive Specification – Currently in its third edition, this helpful standard was developed by RCHME. Besides providing a short overview to field recording practice, this document provides a useful summary of architectural drawing conventions. There is little discussion of digital recording of historic buildings, but many of the recommendations made are also relevant for those using CAD packages.

Towards an Accessible Archaeological Archive. The Transfer of Archaeological Archives to Museums: Guidelines for Use in England, Northern Ireland, Scotland and Wales. The Society of Museum Archaeologists 1995 guide, edited by Janet Owen, provides detailed information about all aspects of preparing an archive for deposit in a museum. Does not cover digital archiving explicitly, but does provide detailed advice on documentary archives with sources of information and a bibliography.